Fodor's InFocus

D0360741

ACAPULCO

1st Edition

Where to Stay and Eat
for All Budgets

Must-See Sights
and Local Secrets

Ratings You Can Trust

Portions of this book appear in *Fodor's Mexico*
Fodor's Travel Publications New York, Toronto, London, Sydney, Auckland
www.fodors.com

FODOR'S IN FOCUS ACAPULCO

Editor: Kelly Lack

Editorial Contributor: Christina Knight

Writers: Carissa Bluestone, Grant Cogswell, Jonathan J. Levin, Claudia Rosenbaum

Editorial Production: Carolyn Roth

Maps & Illustrations: David Lindroth, *cartographer*; Bob Blake, William Wu, and Rebecca Baer, *map editors*

Design: Fabrizio LaRocca, *creative director*; Guido Caroti, *art director*; Ann McBride, *designer*; Melanie Marin, *senior picture editor*

Cover Photo (La Quebrada): World Pictures/Alamy

Production/Manufacturing: Matthew Struble

COPYRIGHT

1st Edition

ISBN 978-1-4000-0759-2

ISSN 1942-7336

SPECIAL SALES

This book is available for special discounts for bulk purchases for sales promotions or premiums. Special editions, including personalized covers, excerpts of existing books, and corporate imprints, can be created in large quantities for special needs. For more information, write to Special Markets/Premium Sales, 1745 Broadway, MD 6-2, New York, NY 10019, or e-mail specialmarkets@randomhouse.com.

AN IMPORTANT TIP & AN INVITATION

Although all prices, opening times, and other details in this book are based on information supplied to us at press time, changes occur all the time in the travel world, and Fodor's cannot accept responsibility for facts that become outdated or for inadvertent errors or omissions. **So always confirm information when it matters,** especially if you're making a detour to visit a specific place. Your experiences—positive and negative—matter to us. If we have missed or misstated something, **please write to us.** We follow up on all suggestions. Contact the In Focus Acapulco editor at editors@fodors.com or c/o Fodor's at 1745 Broadway, New York, NY 10019.

PRINTED IN THE UNITED STATES OF AMERICA

10 9 8 7 6 5 4 3 2 1

Be a Fodor's Correspondent

Your opinion matters. It matters to us. It matters to your fellow Fodor's travelers, too. And we'd like to hear it. In fact, we *need to hear it. When you share your experiences and opinions, you become an active member of the Fodor's community. Here's how you can help improve Fodor's for all of us.

Tell us when we're right. We rely on local writers to give you an insider's perspective. But our writers and staff editors also depend on you. Your positive feedback is a vote to renew our recommendations for the next edition.

Tell us when we're wrong. We update most of our guides every year. But things change. If any of our descriptions are inaccurate or inadequate, we'll incorporate your changes in the next edition and will correct factual errors at fodors.com *immediately*.

Tell us what to include. You probably have had fantastic travel experiences that aren't yet in Fodor's. Why not share them with a community of like-minded travelers? Share your discoveries and experiences with everyone directly at fodors.com. Your input may lead us to add a new listing or a higher recommendation.

Give us your opinion instantly at our feedback center at www.fodors.com/feedback. You may also e-mail editors@fodors.com with the subject line "In Focus Acapulco Editor." Or send your nominations, comments, and complaints by mail to In Focus Acapulco Editor, Fodor's, 1745 Broadway, New York, NY 10019.

Happy Traveling!

Tim Jarrell, Publisher

CONTENTS

ABOUT THIS BOOK

Our Ratings

We wouldn't recommend a place that wasn't worth your time, but sometimes a place is so exceptial that superlatives don't do it justice: you just have to be there to know. These sights, properties, and experiences get our highest rating, **Fodor's Choice** indicated by orange stars throughout this book. Black stars highlight sights and properties we deem **Highly Recommended** places that our writers, editors, and readers praise again and again for consistency and excellence.

Credit Cards

AE, D, DC, MC, V following restaurant and hotel listings indicate whether American Express, Discover, Diners Club, MasterCard, and Visa are accepted.

Restaurants

Unless we state otherwise, restaurants are open for lunch and dinner daily. We mention dress only when there's a specific requirement and reservations only when they're essential or not accepted.

Hotels

Unless we tell you otherwise, you can assume that the hotels have private bath, phone, TV, and air-conditioning. We always list facilities but not whether you'll be charged an extra fee to use them, so when pricing accommodations, find out what's included.

Many Listings

★	Fodor's Choice
★	Highly recommended
✉	Physical address
✛	Directions
⌂	Mailing address
☎	Telephone
🖷	Fax
⊕	On the Web
✉	E-mail
🎫	Admission fee
☉	Open/closed times
Ⓜ	Metro stations
▭	Credit cards

Hotels & Restaurants

🏨	Hotel
⇄	Number of rooms
⚴	Facilities
�🍽	Meal plans
✕	Restaurant
⌸	Reservations
⚡	Smoking
🍺	BYOB
✕🏨	Hotel with restaurant that warrants a visit

Outdoors

⛳	Golf
⛺	Camping

Other

☺	Family-friendly
⇨	See also
✉	Branch address
☞	Take note

WHEN TO GO

Acapulco is one of those places beloved by Mexican nationals who flock to the coast on their vacations during Christmas week, Easter week, and during July and August, staying in beach homes, rented villas, and hotel rooms. This does mean that if you travel during any of these weeks/months, you'll be privy to a unique look at a very local way of life in which people are at their best, relaxed and with friends and family. The restaurants will be lively, the bars filled-to-the-brim, the beaches chock-full of sunbathers. However, most hotels are booked solid during these times, so try to make reservations at least three months in advance. And keep in mind that during Christmas week, prices rise 30%–60% above those in low season; the Mexican Christmas vacation period is compounded by the fact that snowbirds travel down from the United States and Canada around the same time and often roost all winter. If you're allergic to crowds, consider heading down during the months of fall.

Climate

Hot and humid weather prevails in Acapulco, with temperatures hovering remarkably around 31°C (88°F) year-round and sunshine guaranteed virtually every day. During the rainy season, which coincides with summer from June through October, the late afternoon and night often bring welcome, cooling showers, but these typically pass quickly and usually don't affect your travels. Any time of the year is good for a visit really, but perhaps the best is sometime in October or November, right after the rainy season. During this time, the crowds are small, the prices reasonable, and the hills green from the summer rains. As winter and spring roll around, most of the vegetation turns brown. Of course, watching a summer squall out over the Pacific from your hotel balcony, cold beverage in hand, is a singular Mexico experience.

Weather Chart

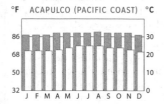

°F   ACAPULCO (PACIFIC COAST)   °C

Chart showing monthly temperatures J F M A M J J A S O N D, with °F axis marked 32, 50, 68, 86 and °C axis marked 0, 10, 20, 30.

Welcome to Acapulco

WORD OF MOUTH

"The western side of the city contains 'old Acapulco.' There we found the famous cliff divers, the zócalo, the flea market, the old fort . . . The northern—more accurately, the middle—part of the city contained the beaches, the hotels, some of the clubs, more restaurants . . . Finally, the eastern side held the big clubs, the fancy restaurants, the spectacular nighttime view of the city's lights, and the large cross overlooking the entire city."

–krbr17

By
Jonathan
J. Levin

1

THE VIEW FROM ANY HOTEL BALCONY ON THE 5-MI ARC COSTERA MIGUEL ALEMÁN tells the story of Acapulco Bay, a tranquil, clear body of water surrounded by a horseshoe of land and civilization, whose villas and dance clubs dot the coastline and climb up into the mountains for an even broader view. More so than any other Mexican resort town, this is a cultural nexus, a place where the big city meets tropical paradise and modern Mexican culture collides with the international tourist experience. Encompassing about a third of the total population of the State of Guerrero, Acapulco is no longer just a remote vacation spot but a major city in its own right.

Five hours from the capital Mexico City, Acapulco is not only a popular port of call for international cruise lines, but also where thousands of chilangos (residents of Mexico City) and other Mexicans have made their second homes. This has led many visitors from abroad to consider Acapulco the most authentically Mexican of the country's major resort towns. Out on the popular commercial strip of "Costera," Spanish is still clearly the language of commerce, and men and women promenade in sexy, forward-looking Latin fashions. Gentlemen, don't forget your white leather shoes. Acapulco also provides a glimpse into the country's flourishing culinary scene, with top chefs combining local tradition with innovative techniques from around the world, frequently served up with a brilliant view of the bay.

As for history, Acapulco was an isolated area until the highway from Mexico City was completed in 1927, purpose-built for tourism. A day trip away is the colonial silver mining town of Taxco, where hundreds of craftsmen and street vendors make it the place to purchase jewelry. Settled by the Aztecs and later by the Spanish army, the city's streets are lined with centuries-old homes and churches, where extravagant religious processions and cultural festivals take place throughout the year. For modern history and pop culture buffs, there are the storied beaches of Acapulco itself, where John and Jacqueline Kennedy spent their honeymoon and Frank Sinatra painted the town with the Rat Pack.

Everyone comes here to celebrate something, if only the good life itself. Many couples plan their "I do's" for this romantic backdrop, American college students raise the volume in all senses during Spring Break, and chilangos crowd the beaches during Semana Santa (Holy Week, or Easter). At dance clubs like Palladium, twenty- and thirty-somethings dance and mingle until around 4:30 am before pouring into an after-hours club like El Classico del Mar, where some will sip champagne until mid-afternoon. During the day, crowds convene around hotel pools and on the golden sand beaches, engaging in cross-cultural conversations or sharing a meal with someone from another part of the globe. Even if you choose to skip the mariachi performances and the Mexican history exhibitions, it's hard to visit Acapulco and not learn something about the country and people that surround you.

Between the 1963 Elvis Presley film, "Fun in Acapulco," and today, a lot has happened for Acapulco and the local economy. For a while, its glamorous Hollywood appeal, begun in the 1950s, disappeared. Its hotels became run down, and the stunning setting lost some of its natural beauty to overdevelopment. But the 1990s changed all that. Careful planning and improved infrastructure have helped facilitate the region's rebirth, and today it's once again the backdrop to popular Mexican films—"Por La Libre" and "Drama/Mex," to name two from the new millenium—and host to world-class hotels, all set before the captivating Acapulco Bay.

TOP REASONS TO GO

Sampling cuisines from around the world, or feasting on classics from throughout Mexico: Dining out is the most popular activity in town, whether it be in a breezy palapa beach shack or an elegant dining room with stunning aerial views of the bay and city lights.

The chance to explore Pie de la Cuesta: This laid-back village northwest of Acapulco on the Pacific Coast is where to slip into authentic small-town life, and to get your fill of fresh, cheap seafood.

Learning about the 500-year history of this seemingly new town: The old Fuerte de San Diego (Fort of San Diego) overlooks Acapulco Bay and houses one of the best museums in Mexico.

Getting out on the town: Acapulco is not a quaint seaside village where the day's activities make for quiet nights. The city comes to life as the sun sets, providing big-city sophistication in fabulous oceanside restaurants, flashy lounges in sleek hotels, dance clubs with a hotter-than-thou clientele, and also laid-back surfer bars on the beach and kitschy, raucous joints.

Shopping for silver: One of Mexico's prettiest colonial towns, Taxco is also the place to buy all things silver—jewelry, ornamentation, cutlery, and much more.

GETTING ORIENTED

The city of Acapulco is on the Pacific coast 433 km (268 mi) south of Mexico City. Warm water, nearly constant sunshine, and balmy year-round temperatures let you plan your day around the beach—whether you want to lounge in a hammock or go snorkeling, parasailing, fishing, or waterskiing. Attractions to lure you away from the sands include crafts markets, cultural institutions, and the amazing cliff divers at La Quebrada.

Old Acapulco. Your trip to Acapulco would be incomplete without a few hours spent exploring the old section. The *zócalo* (town plaza) is filled with majestic banyan and rubber trees, providing shade for a wide cast of characters. The streets are crowded with small businesses and the elusive soul of the city. The beaches are favored by local families and fishermen, now sharing the bay with gigantic cruise ships. The magnificent Fuerte de San Diego is nearby, as is La Quebrada, where otherwise sane men dive more than 30 meters (100 feet) into the surging and rocky Pacific.

Acapulco Bay. Acapulco is the world's largest U-shape outdoor amphitheater, and the Bahía de Acapulco is center stage. The inhabitants in the surrounding hills and beach resorts can admire the action of watercraft and people in the harbor. While the daytime performance is one of fun in the sun, the late-night show features twinkling lights reflected in the water and salsa music drifting on the breeze.

Costera. The heartbeat of Acapulco, Costera pulses with activity. There is nothing quaint or serene about this busy 8-km (5-mi) stretch of commercial bay-front property whose full name is Avenida Costera Miguel Alemán. The thoroughfare is lined with resorts, shops, markets, banks, dance clubs—even a park and a golf course. And within walking distance are the bay's golden beaches. You can land here and never find the need to leave, unless, of course, you crave peace and quiet.

Acapulco Diamante. As you head east from Acapulco Bay you enter Acapulco Diamante, which includes the smaller bay of Puerto Marqués and the long wide beaches of Revolcadero. This is where new developments—mostly large, opulent resorts—crop up. Above, the hillside neighborhoods overlooking the water host many of Mexico's most spectacular private villas. If you like a little breathing room and miles of breezy beach-walking, this is the place for you.

HISTORY

Explanations of the name Acapulco vary among scholars, who have traced the word to a Nahuatl (Aztec language) phrase meaning "place where the reeds were destroyed," or perhaps simply "place of the big reeds." In the better version of the legend, Acatl, the son of a Yope leader, falls in love with Quiahuitl, the daughter of a rival Nahua leader. When their parents forbid them to be together, Acatl cries ceaselessly until he is subsumed by his own tears and flows into a reed-lined pond. Quiahuitl, meanwhile, turns into a cloud and comes to pour down upon the pond every rainy season, compelling the waters to rise up over the reed and form Acapulco Bay.

Hidden at the edge of the mountainous state of Guerrero, Acapulco was for thousands of years inhabited by the Yope, a fierce tribe of Tlapanec-speakers who are believed to be responsible for the 2,000-year-old petroglyphs (cave paintings) in the mountainside northeast of Acapulco, now tourist attractions. Despite the presence of the Aztec-influenced Nahua elsewhere along the Pacific Coast, the Yope appear to have maintained sovereignty over the region, known as Yopitzinco, until the arrival of the Spanish in the mid-16th century.

In 1519 Hernán Cortés made his first trip to the Aztec capital of Tenochtitlán (site of Mexico City) to meet the Aztec emperor Moctezuma II, and initially the two men are believed to have treated each other civilly. (According to the Florentine Codex, a document written some 50 years after these events, the Aztec ruler mistook the explorer's arrival for the return of Quetzalcoatl, an Aztec deity. But many scholars have questioned the accuracy of this account, denying the existence of any pre-Columbian Aztec legend surrounding the return of Quetzalcoatl.) For uncertain motives, the Spanish eventually took Moctezuma II prisoner, during which time Cortés and his men launched their

1

Fun in Acapulco

In the 1963 film "Fun in Acapulco," Elvis Presley plays Mike Windgren, a former circus performer who develops a serious fear of heights after accidentally causing a fellow trapeze artist to get injured on the job. Riddled with guilt, Windgren flees the circus and sets out to create a new life for himself in Mexico. Once in Acapulco, the handsome young man lands a job as a hotel lifeguard, and (of course) spends his nights serenading the guests. In the process he finds himself in the middle of a spicy love triangle with two gorgeous Latin women.

Like Elvis's other movies (this was his 13th), "Fun in Acapulco" was primarily an excuse to have the heartthrob sing and look good on the big screen. Nevertheless, the film thrust Acapulco into the spotlight and inspired a whole new group of single men and women to travel south lured by promises of fun in the sun, and a perpetual beach-party atmosphere. Ironically, Elvis himself filmed all of his scenes for the movie in Hollywood; a double covered for him in the on-location shots. Three years earlier, at the premier of his film "G.I. Blues," a group of Elvis-maniacs had started a riot in a Mexico City movie theater. Consequently, the Mexican government had banned the showing of Elvis movies, making the megastar feel less than welcome in the country's most popular resort town.

---

violent and expansive conquest of his empire. On December 13, 1522, the feast day of Saint Lucy, Spaniard Juan Rodríguez de Villafuerte founded the Pueblo de Villafuerte at what is today known as the Port of Acapulco.

The placid waters of Acapulco Bay made the perfect landing for trade ships from South America, Europe, and Asia, which merchants unloaded of their exotic fabrics and spices and restocked with Mexican silver. By 1617 the Spanish had built the Fortress of San Diego, a military installment complete with powerful canons intended to discourage the pirates who lingered in the Pacific's endless maze of alcoves and canals, waiting to prey on unsuspecting cargo ships. Although the fort sustained major damage in the earthquake of 1776, it stands today, fully restored, as the home of the Museo Histórico de Acapulco.

The Mexican War of Independence officially broke out in 1810, and under José María Morelos, rebels eventually took

Acapulco and nearby Oaxaca from the Spanish. Shortly afterward, Morelos himself was executed for treason, but with the signing of the Treaty of Córdoba, Mexico would take control of its own fate in 1821.

In 1927 the government completed a road between Acapulco and the growing metropolis to the northeast, Mexico City. Thus began the Golden Era of Acapulco. Hotel developers rushed to get a piece of the action, and by the 1950s celebrities were flocking to Acapulco's glamorous new resorts. In 1958 Frank Sinatra popularized "Come Fly with Me," in which he croons, "Just say the words and we'll beat the birds down to Acapulco Bay." The young resort town not only hosted some of the world's great entertainers, it also inspired them.

Since the "Come Fly with Me" years, Acapulco has withstood the vicissitudes of a Mexican tourism industry very much refocused on new resorts in Cancún, Puerto Vallarta, and Los Cabos. But in the wake of a major effort to clean up the bay and attract new investors, leisure travelers and Hollywood big shots alike are once again singing Acapulco's praises.

CULTURE

Although Acapulco's developers have always emphasized Hollywood hedonism over Mexican tradition, the town's culture has come to represent the totality of its rich and diverse population, from its local hospitality workers to its communities of American and European expatriates. And then there are the Mexico City celebrities and businesspeople who have built their second homes here and, in the process, introduced the cosmopolitan niceties of one of the world's largest cities. (Recent statistics estimate Greater Mexico City's population at around 20 million.) In that sense, Acapulco is a small town with big city tastes. Its culinary masters draw on the flavors of Havana and Rome, Bangkok and Cairo; its DJs spin the latest electronic music from Europe and the United States; and its architects conceive space-age restaurants and hotels, where the craftsmanship is outshined only by the view from the balcony.

Acapulco, of course, is a Mexican town first and foremost, and you can't get far without coming across a taquería, or taco shop. The taco is to Mexico as the hamburger is to the United States, and chains like Los Tarascos or the

Wal-Mart-owned VIPS offer what some might call the true modern-day Mexican street food experience, albeit without the best prices or the most personal service in town. But there are still plenty of small restaurants in Acapulco where charming grandmothers prepare everything from scratch, including the tortilla. A walk through El Pueblito, the little market in the heart of the Golden Zone reveals some half-dozen mom-and-pop taquerías, where the food has a home-cooked taste that larger restaurants, especially the chains, simply cannot replicate. Try some shrimp or fried fish tacos, which are among the great payoffs of the marriage between Mexican tradition and coastal life.

In keeping with the town's cosmopolitan spirit, DJs in Acapulco spin the commercial Latin aesthetic heard today across the Americas, from New York City to Buenos Aires. In fact, the majority of today's Latin pop is produced in Mexico by the country's powerhouse entertainment industry, and as a result, Acapulco is often one step ahead of the latest trends. At the same time, it's relatively common to hear traditional Mexican genres like bandera and ranchera playing in restaurants and blaring from car stereos. Much like American country music, these styles are most popular outside of urban centers, and typically come to Acapulco via migrant workers, who have left their rural hometowns in search of a more promising job market.

It's important to remember that Acapulco is a town of travelers and, thus, a town whose culture is constantly in flux. During Semana Santa, or Holy Week (Easter), Mexicans young and old flock to the town to lie in the sand and dance in the clubs. During Spring Break season, groups of American college students pour into hotels and bars with such predictability that many locals now know the dates on which particular universities take their breaks. ("Last week in February," an elderly Acapulco woman was overheard saying in Spanish. "University of Michigan should be here already.") Then there's the respective high seasons for the Japanese and for Europeans. With each influx of tourists, the spirit of Acapulco changes into something slightly different from what it had been just a week earlier—that is what truly defines Acapulco, a town where vacation is a way of life.

LODGING

As Acapulco's status rises among epicureans and urbanites, the demand for all-inclusive packages—which precludes sampling the talents of independent restaurants—has diminished proportionately. Today Acapulco's best new resorts offer their fine spa treatments and dining options à la carte.

Even with some of the region's best-reviewed restaurants right on their premises, the Mayan Palace and the Fairmount Princess both give you the option to explore what's on greater Acapulco's tables. The best choice for families, the Mayan Palace, a Mexican-contemporary take on Hadrian's Villa in Tivoli, boasts its own water park and a 2,625-foot swimming pool, one of the largest in Latin America. The couples friendly Fairmount Princess, in contrast, emphasizes calming gardens and is listed among Golf Digest's "Top 25 Golf Resorts." Both are remote enough to avoid the noise and congestion of the Costera, but their Acapulco Diamante addresses put you only a 25-minute cab ride from the thick of it all.

Closer to town and at the eastern tip of the coast's "horseshoe" bend, Las Brisas is one of the hippest and surprisingly tranquil neighborhoods in the city. On a hillside a short drive from the Costera Miguel Alemán, the winding neighborhood is the site of the serene minimalist Las Brisas Resort, whose earthy ocean-view casitas make it perfect for honeymooners. This is also the place to go for great restaurants, including Baikal, which was considered by some the best in Acapulco until Becco al Mare opened right next door. Among Mexico's wealthy set, this is the most desirable neighborhood in which to build a vacation home, and throughout the year, a number of owners put their lavish villas up for rent, many of them large enough to host up to 12 couples.

Coming from the airport you'll travel westward and pass the naval base tucked in the bay before hitting the Costera Miguel Alemán, often referred to simply as the Costera, the center of all the action. For travelers who want to party every night, this is the place to stay. In the heart of everything, there's the Fiesta Americana, whose recently overhauled rooms are classier than the chain's casual, family-friendly reputation suggests. Be that as it may, the area fills up with college students every spring, who converge on the worn-down hotel on the opposite side of the street, the Romano Palace, for its special rates and proximity to outdoor dance clubs. The Best Western Playa Suites is equally popular among twentysomethings, and unless you're one of them, it should be avoided at all costs during vacation periods.

If you're dead set on an all-inclusive, there are a couple of reasonably priced options along the Costera, most of them out of earshot of the party zone. Despite the mixed reviews they receive from guests, the Ritz (not a Ritz-Carlton) and the Park Royal still manage to fill their rooms with snowbirds, when winter rates are 30%–60% higher than in the spring and summer rainy season. As in other parts of the world, these resorts are most popular among mature travelers.

Finally, there's Old Acapulco, which many of today's tourists overlook with all the development in Las Brisas and Acapulco Diamante (Diamond Zone). Old Acapulco's restaurants and hotels are relics of the city's rich past, and with several of them undergoing much-needed makeovers, the area may finally get a second wind. Facing Isla Roqueta from the mainland, Hotel Boca Chica is an inexpensive, if off-the-beaten-track alternative. The canal in front of the hotel provides for some of the best snorkeling in Acapulco, and the restaurant has excellent sushi. Also nearby, Hotel Mirador Acapulco is host to one of the city's longest-standing traditions, the Cliff Diving Show at La Quebrada. Although the hotel is drab and inconveniently located, the show itself is not to be missed.

IF YOU LIKE

BEACHES

Beaches in Acapulco change with the seasons. During rainy season (May to October), the tide comes right up to the rocks at some expanses. For a little breathing room, your best bet is to head to the broader beaches of Playa Revolcadero, by the Fairmount Princess Hotel. In contrast, the beaches of Old Acapulco (Caleta and Caletilla) are on the small side, but they're always teeming with families. No matter where you go, there's no avoiding the vendors who work most of Acapulco's beaches—legally, they have a right to be there.

Costera Beaches. Playa Hornitos, Playa Morro, Playa Condesa, and Playa Icacos are all part of the same swath of shoreline (from west to east), which is fair game to sunbathers up to the generous border of the naval base. These beaches average 150-feet in depth and are the front yard of many Costera resorts.

Playas Caleta and Caletilla. In the heart of Old Acapulco, these beaches are popular among families and are lined with cheap seafood shacks and share an aquarium.

Playa de Los Hornos. A short walk from the zócalo, Playa de Los Hornos is slightly less hectic for families than Caleta and Caletilla. It's also convenient to a number of budget, mom-and-pop-style hotels.

Playa Revolcadero. This broad swath of oceanfront beach sits in front of Acapulco's most exclusive resorts and is one of the only beaches suitable for surfing.

DINING OUT

Acapulco's best new fine-dining establishments are outside of town in the hills of Las Brisas. Becco al Mare and Baikal, make nearly every critic's best-of Acapulco list. No matter where you eat or how much you plan to spend, seafood dishes are likely to be the best on the menu. For an inexpensive meal that truly embodies coastal Mexican culture, try an order of shrimp or fish tacos.

100% Natural. With locations up and down the Costera, this chain restaurant will surprise you with some of the freshest tasting enchiladas around.

Baikal. This restaurant fuses the unique tastes and textures of France, Asia, and Mexico without sacrificing the integrity of any cuisine.

Becco al Mare. Featured in the New York Times travel section, besides serving delicious meals, this Las Brisas Italian restaurant is one of Acapulco's great accomplishments in modern architecture.

El Amigo Miguel. A favorite among locals, El Amigo Miguel serves up great inexpensive seafood right on the beach.

Jovito's. For seafood tacos, there's no better option in Acapulco. Be sure to sample every one of the nine types of salsa at your table.

EXPLORING THE OUTDOORS

Placid Acapulco Bay is a great place for new or experienced scuba-divers and snorkelers to observe the marine life of the Pacific. The best dive sites are out by Isla Roqueta, where you're likely to see spotted eels and butterfly fish. If you want to explore on your own, without all the trouble of chartering a boat and a guide, jump in by Hotel Boca Chica. For a less daring outdoor activity, a simple moonlighted walk on one of Acapulco's beaches is a great option, too. The wet-sand beaches attract plenty of interesting crustaceans.

Acapulco Scuba Center. For the best off-shore tours and the option of a four-day open-water certification course, check out the offerings of these scuba experts. ⊠ *Paseo del Pescador 13 y 14, Old Acapulco* ☎744/482–9474 ⊕*www. acapulcoscuba.com*

Baby Sea Turtle Reserve. The Mayan Palace is host to a sea turtle preserve, where the hotel's operators work in conjunction with local ecologists to save the turtles from extinction.

Pueblo Bravo Rafting. Book your rafting adventure at this Costera outpost. The guides make sure your trip is fun and safe. ⊠ *Costera Miguel Aleman 121–130* ☎ *744/484–1154*

Viajes Acuario This travel agent is incredibly easy to find, smack in the center of the action on the Costera strip. ⊠ *Av. Costera Miguel Alemán 186–3, Costera* ☎744/485–6100

SPA TREATMENTS

Most of Acapulco's spas are within resorts and offer similar massages and skin-care treatments, with a few noteworthy exceptions. Bambuddha, for instance, offers a traditional Maya ceremony called temazcal, in which aromatherapy is administered in a pitch-black sweat lodge. Like everything else in Acapulco, the best spas fill their appointment books quickly, especially during peak times of the year. It's always best to book in advance.

Alory Spa. This spa in the Hyatt Regency offers a variety of mud and eucalyptus treatments, including the Mayan Mud Wrap.

Bambuddha. In addition to a temazcal, this elegant spa offers herbal baths and meditation. ⊠ *Carretera a Barra Vieja s/n km. 37.5, San Andrés.* ☎ *744/444-6406.*

Villa Vera Spa & Racquet Club. With one of the most extensive lists of treatments and the most qualified staff, this spa is best known for its deep cleaning European facials.

Willow Stream Spa. This spa in the Fairmont Acapulco Princess promises to energize your skin with its Latin Latte treatment, which combines an exfoliation with a coffee-based mud wrap.

GREAT ITINERARY

Spend a few morning hours sunning at either **Playa Revolcadero**, in front of the Fairmount Princess Hotel, or **Playa Caleta**, in Old Acapulco. The former has big waves and makes for decent surfing, while the latter is close to the zócalo, where you can head for shopping during the afternoon. Nearby the **Mercado de Artesanías El Parazal** has a great assortment of vendors selling everything from jewelry to Oaxaca black pottery, and while you're out, you might want to try some of the local cocadas and tamarindos, the wildly popular local candies made from real fruit. For a more substantial afternoon snack, stop into a taquería for an order of tacos al pastor prepared on a vertical rotisserie and served with onions, pineapple, and cilantro.

After unloading your purchases at the hotel, head out to a spa for a mid-afternoon body treatment, like the deeply hydrating Mayan Mud Wrap at the Hyatt Regency's **Alory Spa**. (Ideally, you will have booked at least a day in advance, hint hint.) When the treatment is over, you'll be well primed for a late-afternoon nap, which you're going to need if you have any intention of partaking in Acapulco's nightlife.

When dressing for the evening, remember that local restaurants and dance clubs generally have a more formal standard of dress than their American counterparts. Men and women should wear leather shoes, not sneakers or sandals. If you're traveling with small children, you should consider dinner at Acapulco's favorite theme restaurant, **Carlos and Charlie's**, whose walls are adorned with enough visual noise to make TGI Fridays look like a project in minimalism.

Young or just young at heart, it would be a shame for anyone to visit Acapulco and not enjoy at least one night on the town. Along the Costera the dance clubs play everything from salsa to hip-hop. For young singles no party experience compares to **Palladium**, the überdisco set on a hillside in Las Brisas, whose glass walls allow patrons to admire all of Acapulco while dancing to what is probably the most powerful sound system in the State of Guerrero. If noisy dance clubs aren't your thing, consider a walk along the beach, where groups of friends gather to steal a dip in the still-warm bay and lone mariachis can be heard rehearsing for the next day's performance.

Exploring Acapulco

WORD OF MOUTH

"Make sure you go see the cliff divers. And, the best way to see them is to rent a speed boat from in front of your hotel (they are available everywhere), and then travel to see the divers from the sea. It is a terrific site and well worth the time and small effort."

—tengohambre

Updated by Claudia Rosenbaum

THE CENTER OF ACAPULCO IS ON THE WESTERN EDGE OF THE BAY. The streets form a grid that's easy to explore on foot. Avenida Costera Miguel Alemán, a wide coastal boulevard, runs the length of the bay and is lined with hotels, restaurants, and malls. You can explore the strip by taxi, bus, or rental car, stopping along the way to shop.

2

You'll also need a vehicle to get to Acapulco Diamante, farther east along the coast. Running from Las Brisas Hotel to Barra Vieja beach, this 3,000 acre expanse encompasses exclusive Playa Diamante and Playa Revolcadero, with upscale hotels and residential developments, private clubs, beautiful views, and pounding surf.

Pie de la Cuesta, 10 km (6.2 mi) northwest of Acapulco, is famous for its fabulous sunsets, small family-run hotels, and some of the wildest surf in Mexico. The village remains the flip side to the Acapulco coin—a welcome respite from the disco-driven big city. Only the main road is paved, and the town has no major resorts or late-night clubs. A beach chair, a bucket of cold beers, fresh fish and seafood, and a good book is about as much excitement as you'll get here.

For a break from beach life you can travel north 300 km (185 mi) to the old silver-mining town of Taxco, a great place to buy silver from the country's finest metalwork artisans.

GETTING AROUND

If you're in town for a long weekend and want to spend most of your time beachside, don't bother renting a car. A small army of taxis and buses is ready to whisk you along the Costera and anywhere else you want to go in town. Taxis are relatively cheap—a ride from Acapulco Diamante to downtown will cost you about $15. If you want to visit the coastal villages and Taxco, however, consider renting a car or open-air jeep, or taking a coach. You can rent a car for $30 per day, including insurance and unlimited miles. And did we mention that the jeeps come in bright pink?

COSTERA

Avenida Costera Miguel Alemán hugs the Bahía de Acapulco from the Carretera Escénica (Scenic Highway) in the east to Playa Caleta (Caleta Beach) in the southwest—a distance of about 8 km (5 mi). Most of the major beaches, shopping malls, and hotels are along or off this avenue, and locals refer to its most exclusive stretch—from El Presidente

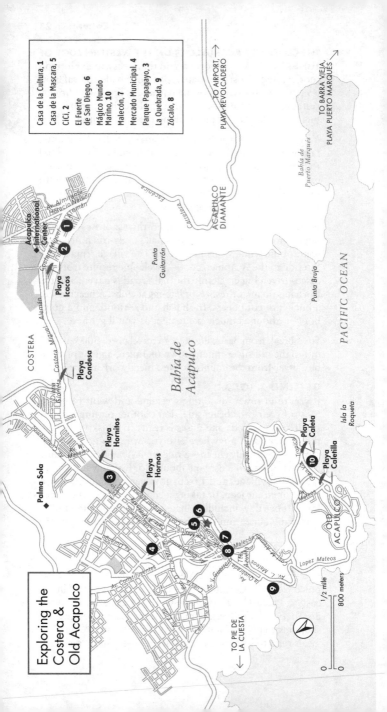

Exploring the Costera & Old Acapulco

Casa de la Cultura, **1**
Casa de la Mascara, **5**
CiCi, **2**
El Fuerte de San Diego, **6**
Mágico Mundo Marino, **10**
Malecón, **7**
Mercado Municipal, **4**
Parque Papagayo, **3**
La Quebrada, **9**
Zócalo, **8**

TO AIRPORT, PLAYA REVOLCADERO →

TO BARRA VIEJA, PLAYA PUERTO MARQUES ↗

Bahía de Puerto Marques

ACAPULCO DIAMANTE

Punta Guitarrón

Punta Bruja

PACIFIC OCEAN

Bahía de Acapulco

Isla la Roqueta

Playa Caleta

Playa Caletilla

OLD ACAPULCO

Lopez Mateos

Playa Icacos

Playa Condesa

COSTERA

Playa Hornitos

Playa Hornos

Palma Sola

Acapulco International Center

Av. Almirante Horacio Nelson

Costera Miguel Alemán

Diana Glorieta

A. W. Mateos

TO PIE DE LA CUESTA ↖

Av. Constituyentes

1/2 mile

800 meters

0

0

hotel to Las Brisas—simply as "the Costera." Since many addresses are listed as only "Costera Miguel Alemán," you'll need good directions from a major landmark to find specific shops and hotels.

WHAT TO SEE

1 Casa de la Cultura. The city's cultural center has first-class regional and Mexican handicrafts for sale, the Ixcateopan art gallery, and a small sports hall of fame with photos of local athletes. The center also sponsors folk dancing and theater productions, and offers language workshops. ⊠*Av. Costera Miguel Alemán 4834, Costera* ☎*744/484–2390* ☜*Free* ☉*Daily 8 AM–9 PM.*

2 CiCi. A water park for children, the Centro Internacional para Convivencia Infantil, fondly known as CiCi, has dolphin shows, a freshwater pool with a wave machine, a waterslide, the Sky Coaster (a safe, low-key bungee jump for kids), and other attractions. If you book an hour-long swim with the dolphins, CiCi can have you picked up at your hotel. It's easy to catch a cab for the return trip. ⊠*Av. Costera Miguel Alemán, next to Planet Hollywood, Costera* ☎*744/484–1970* ☜*$10* ☉*Daily 10–6.*

VINTAGE TOURING. Horse-drawn carriage rides, known as calandrias, run up and down the Costera in the evenings and can be a fun way to get to a restaurant or club. There are several routes, including one from Parque Papagayo to the zócalo (town square) and another from Playa Condesa to the naval base. Rides cost $7.50–$14, depending on the route. Be sure to agree on the price beforehand.

3 Parque Papagayo. Named for the hotel that formerly occupied the grounds, this park is on 52 acres of prime Costera real estate, just after the underpass that begins at Playa Hornos. It has an aviary, a racetrack with mite-size race cars, a space-shuttle replica, a jogging path, a library, and bumper boats. Find some street food and a shady bench and do some people-watching. ⊠*Av. Costera Miguel Alemán, Costera* ☎*744/485–6837* ☜*No entrance fee; rides $1 each; $5 ride packages available* ☉*Park: daily 6 AM–8 PM. Rides section: nightly 4–11.*

OLD ACAPULCO

Old Acapulco, an area that you can easily tour on foot, is where the locals go to dine, enjoy a town festival, run errands, and worship. Also known as El Centro, it's where you'll find the zócalo, the church, and El Fuerte de San Diego. Although a very old city, Acapulco retains little in the way of centuries-old buildings. When development took off here in the '40s and '50s many of the old buildings were razed to make room for resort hotels.

WHAT TO SEE

❺ Casa de la Mascara. A private home has been turned into a gallery for a stunning collection of 550 handmade ceremonial masks, most from the state of Guerrero. Some are representative of those still used in such traditional ritualistic dances as "Moors and Christians" and "Battle of the Tigers." Call ahead to book a 30-minute tour in English or Spanish. ✉ *Calle Morelos s/n, Ex-Zona Militar B, a half block from Fuerte de San Diego, Old Acapulco* ☎744/485–3944 or 744/485–3404 ⬛*Free* ☉*Tues.–Sat.* 10–5.

TAKE THE TROLLEY. An open-air trolley, called the *tranvía*, is convenient for touring the major attractions along the Costera and in Old Acapulco. Operating daily 10–6, the trolley starts at the Parque Papagayo and stops at the Fuerte de San Diego, La Quebrada, Caleta beach, the zócalo, the convention center, and at most hotels along the Costera up until the Hyatt ($6.50 for unlimited rides in one day).

❻ Fodor's Choice **El Fuerte de San Diego.** Acapulco's fort was built ★ in 1616 to protect the city's lucrative harbor and wealthy citizens from pirate attacks. Although it was badly damaged by an earthquake in 1776, it was entirely restored by the end of that century. Today the fort houses the excellent **Museo Histórico de Acapulco** *(Acapulco History Museum).* Bilingual videos and text explain exhibits tracing the city's history from the first pre-Hispanic settlements 3,000 years ago through the exploits of pirates like Sir Francis Drake, the era of the missionaries, and up to Mexico's independence from Spain in 1821. There are also displays of precious silks, Talavera tiles, exquisitely hand-tooled wooden furniture, and delicate china. A good multimedia show in Spanish (an English version requires a minimum of 15 people) on the history of Acapulco is staged outside the museum grounds on Thursday, Friday, and Saturday at 8

PM for $10 per person. A visit to the fort is a wonderful way to learn about and appreciate the history of this old port city. ⊠*Calle Hornitos and Calle Morelos, Old Acapulco*☎744/482–3828 ☜*$3.60, free on Sunday* ⊗*Tues.–Sun. 9:30–6.*

Palma Sola. Taking the name of the neighborhood closest to it, this archaeological site juts up a mountainside northeast of Old Acapulco. The area is blanketed with 2,000-year-old petroglyphs executed by the Yopes, Acapulco's earliest known inhabitants. Stone steps with intermittent plazas for viewing the ancient art are set along a path through virgin vegetation. A cave used as a ceremonial center is atop the mountain, more than 1,000 feet above sea level and definitely worth the visit. It's about a 25-minute taxi ride from Old Acapulco. ☎744/486–1514 for tours ☜*Free* ⊗*Daily 8–4.*

❿ **Mágico Mundo Marino.** You can take in Magic Marine World's aquarium and free sea-lion show while the kids splash around in the swimming pools and fly down the waterslides. From Playa Caleta you can take the glass-bottom boat to Isla la Roqueta—about 10 minutes each way—for snorkeling. ⊠*Islote de Caleta, Old Acapulco*☎744/483–1193 ☜*$6 for adults, $3 for children. Round-trip boat ride to Isla la Roqueta $5* ⊗*Daily 9–6.*

❼ **Malecón.** A stroll by the docks will confirm that Acapulco is a lively port. At night Mexicans bring their children to play on the tree-lined promenade. Farther west, by the zócalo, are docks for yachts and fishing boats. ⊠*Av. Costera Miguel Alemán between Calle Escudero on the west and El Fuerte de San Diego on the east, Old Acapulco.*

❹ **Mercado Municipal.** Locals come to this municipal market to buy everything from candles and fresh vegetables to plastic buckets and love potions. In addition, you can buy baskets, pottery, hammocks—there's even a stand offering charms, amulets, and talismans. The stalls within the mercado are densely packed together and there's no air-conditioning, but things stay relatively cool. Come early to avoid the crowds. ⊠*Calle Diego Hurtado de Mendoza and Av. Constituyentes, a few blocks west of Costera, Old Acapulco* ⊗*Daily 5* AM–*7* PM.

BAY BONANZA. A lovely way to see the bay is to sign up for a cruise on the *Fiesta & Bonanza* (☎744/483–1803). Boats leave from downtown near the zócalo at 11 AM, 4:30 PM, and 10:30 PM. The evening cruise includes live Latin- or disco music and dancing, and an open bar with domestic alcohol. Many hotels and shops sell tickets ($31.50), as do waterfront ticket sellers.

9 La Quebrada. Just up the hill from Old Acapulco is the southern peninsula, where you'll find this cliff and its legendary divers. The peninsula has remnants of Acapulco's golden era, the early- to mid-20th century. Although past its prime, this mostly residential area has been revitalized through the reopenings of the Caleta Hotel and the aquarium at Playa Caleta. And the inexpensive hotels here are still popular with travelers who want good deals and a slower pace. The Plaza de Toros, where bullfights are held on Sunday from the first week of January to Easter, is in the center of the peninsula.

8 Zócalo. Old Acapulco's hub is this shaded plaza overgrown with dense trees. All day it's filled with vendors, shoe-shine men, and tourists enjoying the culture. After siesta, the locals drift here to socialize. On Sunday evening there's often music in the bandstand. The zócalo fronts Nuestra Señora de la Soledad (Our Lady of Solitude), the town's modern but unusual church, with its stark-white exterior and bulb-shape blue-and-yellow spires. The church hosts the festive Virgin of Guadalupe celebration on December 12. ⊠*Bounded by Calle Felipe Valle on the north, Av. Costera Miguel Alemán on the south, Calle J. Azueta on the west, and Calle J. Carranza on the east, Old Acapulco.*

Where to Stay

WORD OF MOUTH

"We tried to brush up on our basic Spanish: our P's and Q's, directions, numbers, colors, meals, etc. This was needed for Acapulco more so than other destinations in Mexico because Acapulco is where Mexicans go for vacation, and thus knowledge of English is less of a necessity for the people who work there because many of their customers are Mexican."

—krbr17

By Grant
Cogswell
&
Jonathan
J. Levin

IT'S THE TRANQUIL WATERS OF ACAPULCO BAY that spawned the town's development almost a century ago, but if it's peace and quiet you're after, be careful where you choose to stay. The Costera offers the only all-inclusives (which are hardly desirable now that the city's restaurant scene is hopping) and a party-hearty energy. Bars and clubs on the Costera Miguel Alemán rage through the week and into the wee hours, making it the obvious stomping grounds of young Mexicans and American college students on spring break.

If you set your sights beyond the Costera, you'll find lodging options that provide greater variety in price and ambience. The large, establishments in Acapulco Diamante, out east near the airport, are somewhat isolated, set in a landscape of golf courses and palm groves, with restaurants and shops within the hotel grounds.

Beachcombers in Barra Vieja (to the east) and Pie de la Cuesta (to the west) will find cozy, tropical hideaways. Two exquisite boutique hotels gracing the Barra Vieja—Yal'ma Ka'an and Villas San Vicente—are unsurpassed for quality on the outskirts of town. If you're low on funds, consider Old Acapulco's selection of funky, cheap (but clean) establishments from the resort's early glory days. Acapulco mainstays like Hotel Boca Chica, on the Canal Boca Chica, offer unique access points to the bay. Old Acapulco is less crowded than the Costera, with better budget restaurants and a casual, friendly community of North American snowbirds. Deals can be made with the more expensive places if you're willing to book far in advance, or stay off-season or midweek.

ABOUT THE HOTELS

Hotels on the Costera run the gambit in terms of quality and price, from lavish chains to individually owned and run establishments, where you might have to knock loudly on the gate to gain access after midnight. The vast majority of hotels accept credit cards, but if you decide to stay at a place with fewer than 50 rooms or in Old Acapulco or Pie de la Cuesta, ask first before you arrive without cash.

Off the Costera, hotels range from an incredible $15 a night in humble two- and three-story lodgings near Old Acapulco`s zócalo, up to $600 a night in the luxury accommodations in Acapulco Diamante. Rooms in the hotels listed here have private bathrooms and provide a pitcher of purified water, bottled water, or have a cooler in the lobby.

Acapulco's pollution and water-quality issues improved with the massive infrastructure overhaul it underwent in the 1990s, but it's best not to risk drink the tap water—not even the locals do.

Many North Americans, after testing the waters for a week or two in Acapulco, decide to spend longer stretches of time to enjoy the near-perfect climate, beaches, and affordable living. That's why, in addition to its more than 20,000 hotel rooms, the city and surrounding area has just as many condominiums, and their numbers are growing fast. Luckily, the town is so big and the tourist trade so internationally diverse that you aren't likely to suffer a deluge of pitchmen selling timeshares.

3

If you're considering investing in a condo, locals suggest poking around and making inquiries: if you see a building that looks like it could be a hotel, but with no advertising on it or taxi drivers out front, it's likely a condo. They're all over, from the hills above Caleta—a surprisingly cheap area, and conveniently close-in—to the Costera and the little cul-de-sacs off the Carretera Escènica, and behind Puerto Marqués and Barra Vieja (condos haven't touched down in Pie de la Cuesta yet). Usually at these places, should you find one that takes your fancy, you'll find a resident or maintenance person who can give you basic information. Prices are all over the map, from as little as $300 a month for long stays, and on the top end the sky is the limit.

WHAT IT COSTS IN U.S. DOLLARS				
¢	$	$$	$$$	$$$$
HOTELS				
under $50	$50–$75	$75–$150	$150–$250	over $250

Hotel prices are for two people in a standard double room in high season.

If you're going to be an Acapulco regular, condos are a much better bargain than staying in hotels. The most popular online resource for condo seekers is ⊕*www.ronlavender. com*. While in the city, you might try the following: **Costa Diamante** ⊠*Av. Costera Miguel Alemàn 81, La Condesa* ☎*744/435–2525;* **Lucunza y Asociados** ⊠*Av. Costera Miguel*

Alemàn 1632, Costa Azul ☎744/486–8677; **Realty Mex**
✉*Calle Alonso Martìn 43, Centro* ☎744/485–9090.

THE COSTERA

The 8-km (5-mi) stretch of Avenida Costera Miguel Alemán
known as the Costera is lined with beachfront backed by
tightly packed high-rise hotels. Most were built in the '60s
and '70s, forever changing one of the world's most beautiful bays. The hotels are in all price categories, the cheaper
properties being on the north side of the avenue. Stay here
if you want to be in the middle of the action, surrounded
by restaurants, bars, discos, shops, malls, and food stores.
For cheap transportation along the Costera, simply jump
on one of the local buses that chug up and down the strip
(a ride costs 4.50 pesos), or flag one of the many taxis.

$$$$ ⚏**Elcano.** Restored to its original 1950s glamour, this peren-
nial favorite has snappy rooms with white-tile floors and
modern bathrooms. There's a beachside restaurant with
an outstanding breakfast buffet, a more elegant indoor
restaurant, and a gorgeous pool that not only seems to
float above the bay, but also has whirlpools built into its
corners. **Pros:** Ocean-facing rooms have balconies, located
on a good stretch of beach. **Cons:** Pool fills up with parents
and kids, exercise room is very small. ✉*Av. Costera Miguel
Alemán 75, Costera* ☎744/435–1500 ⊕*www.hotel-elcano.
com* ⇥*163 rooms, 17 suites* ⚏*In-room: Safe, refrigerator, Wi-Fi. In-hotel: Restaurant, room service, bars, pool,
gym, beachfront, water sports, concierge, laundry service.*
▭*AE, MC, V.*

> **WORD OF MOUTH.** "My friend and I went to Acapulco in January.
> We are in our 50's and also stayed at Fiesta Americana in their
> wonderful one bedroom suite ... what a wonderful view we had
> from our two balconies ... I have been to Rio De Janiero and
> the view is so similar. Also the view of the bay from the pool is
> another breath taking experience." –gizmo

$$$–$$$$ ⚏**Fiesta Americana Villas Acapulco.** In the thick of the main
shopping and restaurant district, this hotel is popular with
tour groups and singles. It has a lively lobby bar and is on
Playa Condesa, one of the most popular beaches in town.
Guest rooms have been overhauled and suites now have
large, lavish kitchens, huge flat-screen TVs in both rooms,
and two balconies. **Pros:** Bar can be loud late at night, good

CLOSE UP

Saying "I do" in Acapulco

Banquetes Acapulco ☎744/404–0239 ⊕www.banquetesacapulco.com

Banquetes Baikal ☎744/446–6845 ⊕www.baikal.com.mx

Banquetes Elcano ☎744/435–1500 ⊕www.hotel-elcano.com

Banquetes Estua ☎744/484–8586 ⊕www.banquetesestua.com

Banquetes Olquin ☎744/485–3915 ⊕www.banquetesolguin.com

Banquetes Susana Palazuelos ☎744/484–1860 ⊕www.susannapalazuelos.com

Caty Gomez Eventos Exclusivos ☎744/484–3663 ⊕www.catygomez.com

Acarey Fun Cruises ☎744/482–3763 🖷744/482–3767 ✍acarey_ventas@yahoo.com.mx.

location. **Cons:** Beach can fill up. ✉*Av. Costera Miguel Alemán 97, Costera* ☎744/435–1600, 800/343–7821 *in U.S.* ⊕*www.fiestaamericana.com* ⤳*492 rooms, 8 suites* ⚴*In-room: Refrigerator, Wi-Fi (some). In-hotel: 2 restaurants, room service, bar, pools, beachfront, water sports, concierge, children's programs (ages 4–12), laundry service.* ▤*AE, MC, V.*

$$$ 📺 **Hyatt Regency Acapulco.** The Hyatt is popular with business travelers, conventioneers, and—thanks to its bold Caribbean color schemes and striking design—TV producers, who have opted to use it as the setting for many a Mexican soap opera. It has four outstanding eateries (one of them a kosher restaurant), the Alory spa, and a deluxe shopping area. It's also the only hotel in Latin America with an on-site synagogue. The west side of the property insulates you from the noise of the nearby naval base. **Pros:** Great service, spacious rooms. **Cons:** Some rooms need updating. ✉*Av. Costera Miguel Alemán 1, Costera* ☎744/469–1234, 800/633–7313 *in U.S. and Canada* ⊕*www.hyatt.com* ⤳*640 rooms, 17 suites* ⚴*In-room: Refrigerator. In-hotel: 4 restaurants, room service, bars, tennis courts, pools, gym, spa, beachfront, children's programs (ages 8–12; high season only), laundry service, parking (no fee), public Internet.* ▤*AE, MC, V.*

$$$ 📺 **Villas La Lupita.** Two blocks from Playa Malibú, Villas La Lupita is a cozy, basic option with cheery little rooms and a bilingual staff. Martha the general manager is friendly and a true perfectionist when it comes to the hotel's maintenance.

There's a small pool and the action of Costera is a block away. **Pros:** Convenient to beach, friendly and personal service. **Cons:** Not many amenities. ✉*Cap. Antón de Alaminos 232, Golden Zone* ☎*744/486–3917* ⊕*www.villaslalupita. com* ⤢*34 rooms* &*In-room: Safe.* ▤*MC, V.*

$$–$$$ 🏨**Bali Hai.** Right in the middle of the hip center of Acapulco, Bali Hai smacks of another era, right down to the faux-bamboo sign that adorns the front of the property. Considering the outdated design and the lack of a view—in the motel tradition, there are only two floors of rooms—the prices are a little steep, even with the hotel's convenient location close to several malls and restaurants. Nevertheless, the service is still of a high caliber and the pool area, which is shaded by palm trees, serves as a pleasant place to unwind. **Pros:** Relaxing pool area, convenient to mall shopping. **Cons:** Outdated design, no view. ✉*Av. Costera Miguel Alemán 186, Golden Zone* ☎*744/485–6622* ⊕*www.balihai. com.mx* ⤢*120 rooms* &*In-room: Refrigerator (some). In-hotel: Restaurant, bar, pool.*▤*AE, D, MC, V.*

$$–$$$ 🏨**Ritz Acapulco.** Not related to the Ritz-Carlton chain, the small Ritz Acapulco's two towers look a bit dated and the experience is more about convenience than luxury. The hotel's bright yellow and blue color scheme can come off as kitschy, but it's really the gorgeous view of the Bay of Santa Lucia that people spend time contemplating. Among Acapulco's all-inclusive options, the Ritz is a well-priced option, especially for mature vacationers—the resort attracts very few families and college students. Prices include breakfast, lunch, and dinner buffets, which feature international and local dishes, as well as an open bar (domestics liquor and beer brands only) from 10 am to midnight. **Pros:** Tranquil atmosphere, inexpensive. Prices include breakfast, lunch, and dinner buffets, which feature international and local dishes, as well as an open bar (domestics only) from 10 am to midnight. **Cons:** Small resort, average rooms. <✉*Costera Miguel Alemán 159, Golden Zone* ☎*744/469–3500* ⊕*www.ritzacapulco.com.mx* ⤢*240 rooms* &*In-hotel: Bar, spa, pool.* ▤*AE, MC, V* ⏹*AI.*

$$–$$$ 🏨**Villa Vera.** A five-minute drive into the hills north of the
★ Costera leads to the place where Elizabeth Taylor married Mike Todd and where Lana Turner settled for three years. This is as close as you can get to the glamour and style of Acapulco when it was Hollywood's retreat. Some villas

Where to Stay in Acapulco

Alba Suites, 1
Bali Hai, 18
Best Western Playa Suites, 22
Boca Chica, 2
Las Brisas, 29
Camino Real Acapulco Diamante, 36
Casa de Huespedes Sutter, 6
Casa Yalma Ka'an, 37
Club del Sol, 17
Crowne Plaza, 21
Elcano, 27
Etel Suites, 5
Fairmont Acapulco Princess, 34
Fairmont Pierre Marqués, 33
Fiesta Americana Villas Acapulco, 25
Fiesta Inn, 26
Los Flamingos, 3
Hacienda Tayma, 9

Las Hamacas, 14
Hostal Kingdom, 35
Hotel Alameda, 8
Hotel Casa Blanca, 12
Hotel Gabachines, 31
Hotel Itto, 15
Hotel Terrazas, 30
Hyatt Regency Acapulco, 28
El Mirador, 4
Misión, 7
Parador del Sol, 10
Park Hotel & Tennis Center, 20
Playa Suave, 13
Quinta Real, 32
Ritz Acapulco, 19
Romano Palace, 23
Villas La Lupita, 16
Villas San Vicente, 38
Villas Ukae Kim, 11
Villa Vera, 24

were once private homes and have their own pools. The excellent Villa Vera Spa and Fitness Center, open to guests and nonguests, has exercise machines, free weights, milk baths, algae treatments, and massages. **Pros:** Architecturally intriguing, extremely comfortable beds. **Cons:** Not near the beach. ⊠*Calle Lomas del Mar 35, Costera* ⌂*A. P. 560 39690* ☎*744/484–0333 or 888/554–2361* ⊕*www. raintreevacationclub.com* ↘*24 rooms, 25 suites, 6 villas* ⌂*In-room: Refrigerator, VCR, Wi-Fi. In-hotel: Restaurant, bar, tennis courts, pools, gym, spa, concierge, no elevator, laundry service, Internet.* ⊟*AE, MC, V* ⁑*EP.*

$$ ⌦**Best Western Playa Suites.** A decent all-inclusive budget option, the hotel offers comfortable accommodation and sufficiently attentive service, but the hotel itself has seen better days. There are rooms with balconies facing the bay. During Spring Break season, Best Western runs promotions for college kids and the resort turns into a PG-13 version of "Girls Gone Wild" and youth take advantage of the alcohol included in the all-inclusive package. Guests that don't plan to participate in the mayhem should avoid it at all costs. **Pros:** Social atmosphere, convenient for shopping and partying. **Cons:** Extremely rowdy hallways during college breaks. ⊠*Av. Costera Miguel Alemán 123, Golden Zone* ☎*744/485–8050* ⊕*www.playasuites.com.mx* ↘*502 rooms* ⌂*In-room: Safe, Wi-Fi. In-hotel: 2 restaurants, room service, pool, parking (no fee).* ⊟*AE, MC, V.*

$$–$$$ ⌦**Crowne Plaza.** With four restaurants on the premises, the Crowne Plaza lets you choose between an all-inclusive and a pay-as-you-go dining plan. It isn't the luxury hotel it once was, but this beachside resort still gives you what you pay for. Every room comes with a view of the bay, but it's worth insisting on a "great" view, as not all balconies are created equal. Some of those staying here are actually on business; the eight meeting halls can accommodate from 50 to 1,200 people. **Pros:** Central location, solid value. **Cons:** Service is below par. ⊠*Av. Costera Miguel Alemán 123, Golden Zone* ☎*744/440–5555* ⊕*www.crowneplaza. com* ↘*348 rooms, 79 suites* ⌂*In-room: Safe. In-hotel: 4 restaurants, 8 pools, beachfront, laundry service, gym, parking (fee).* ⊟*AE, MC, V.*

$$ ⌦**Fiesta Inn.** Owned and operated by the same company as the Fiesta Americana, Fiesta Inn offers a high level of comfort and service without the touristy amenities of its sister hotel. For those who can do without the poolside

DJ and generally nonstop stimulation, the Fiesta Inn is a great place to stay in the heart of the commercial district. The hotel also offers special services to business travelers, like the option to pre-order your breakfast before you go to bed. **Pros:** Quiet hallways, walking distance to popular restaurants, great breakfast buffet. **Cons:** Antisocial clientele, small gym with outdated equipment. ⊠*Costera Miguel Alemán 2311, Golden Zone* ☎*744/435–0500* ⊕*www. fiestainn.com* ⇨*215 rooms, 4 suites* ⚭*In-room: Ethernet. In-hotel: Restaurant, pool, room service, gym, meeting room, business center.* ⊟*AE, MC, V* .

$$ ⌘**Park Hotel & Tennis Center.** A helpful staff and a prime location make this an appealing place to stay. Rooms, which have colonial-style furnishings, are around a garden with a good-size pool. Some have kitchenettes and balconies; all are spotlessly clean. The Park has a tennis center and is only a block from the beach. **Pros:** Good location, fairly inexpensive. **Cons:** Rooms are "economical," hotel bar is tiny. ⊠*Av. Costera Miguel Alemán 127, Costera* ⌐*A.P. 269, 39670*☎*744/485–5992* ⊕*www.parkhotel-acapulco. com* ⇨*88 rooms* ⚭*In-room: Kitchenettes (some). In-hotel: Bar, tennis courts, pool, no elevator, parking (no fee).* ⊟*AE, MC, V* ⭘*EP.*

$–$$ ⌘**Club del Sol.** Close to great beaches and shopping, Club del Sol is an economically sound choice for families or couples. On the seventh-floor terrace, there's a lounge and sun bar featuring two adults-only pools and a pair of Jacuzzis. Despite the dated bedding, the spacious rooms provide refuge from the Acapulco sun, and the staff is constantly on its toes. There's a squash court, a small gym with treadmills and adjoining steam room. While not the cream of Acapulco nightlife, Club del Sol even has its own dance club, Club Círculos Disco Bar. Between January and March, there's an all-inclusive option, which includes three buffet meals daily and unlimited drinks through 11 pm. **Pros:** Great price, spacious rooms. **Cons:** Dated furnishings. ⊠*Av. Costera Miguel Alemán, corner R Reyes Católicos s/n, Fracc. Magallanes* ☎*744/486–6600* ⊕*www.hotelesclub delsol.com.mx* ⇨*380 rooms* ⚭*In-room: Safe. In-hotel: Restaurant, bar, pools, gym.* ⊟*AE, MC, V.*

$–$$ ⌘**Las Hamacas.** Rooms at this friendly 1950s Acapulco hotel surround a large inner courtyard. It's across the street from the beach, a 10-minute walk from downtown, and has a lovely garden of coconut palms. The spacious, light-filled rooms have contemporary wood furniture. Junior suites sleep two adults and two children. A stay here gets you access to a beach club. **Pros:** Nice landscaping, good rates. **Cons:** Accommodations are basic, near cruise ship terminal. ⊠*Av. Costera Miguel Alemán 239, Costera* ☎*744/483–7006* ⊕*www.hamacas.com.mx* ⤳*107 rooms, 20 suites* ⌂*In-hotel: Restaurant, room service, bar, pools, laundry service, parking (no fee).* ▤*MC, V* ❍❘*EP.*

$ ▣**Romano Palace.** Directly across the street from several popular party spots and Acapulco's famous bungee jumping platform, Romano Palace is yet another fun—or aggravating—option during Spring Break and other college holidays. The balconies have terrific views of the popular party strip and the beach. To the hotel's detriment, the rooms are rather outdated, and the lobby isn't quite as "classic" as some hotel personnel may lead you to believe. The tanning deck, on the other hand, is a great place for young singles to meet up. **Pros:** Great views, convenient location. **Cons:** Drab rooms, loud clientele. ⊠ *Costera Miguel Alemán 130, Golden Zone* ☎*744/484–7730* ⊕*www.romanopalace.com. mx* ⤳*252 rooms, 18 suites* ⌂*In-room: Refrigerator. In-hotel: Restaurant, bar, room service, pool, laundry service, public Internet.* ▤*AE, MC, V.*

¢–$ ▣**Hotel Itto.** This hotelito, or "little hotel," has little to offer in the way of a view or ambience, although the Mediterranean color scheme in the rooms is pleasant. The hotel is a short walk from plenty of beaches and shopping. Within its price range, this may be the best-kept little property in Acapulco—clearly, Hotel Itto's new owners are out to win a few loyal customers. **Pros:** Exceptionally clean, cheery colors. **Cons:** No view, no amenities. ⊠*Andres de Urdaneta 14, Parque Papagayo* ☎*744/131–3568* ⤳*22 rooms* ▤*No credit cards.*

¢ ▣**Playa Suave.** Playa Suave is one of the most frugal options around town. With two people in a room, you'll actually pay less here than if you were to stay at one of the local youth hostels, and you'll have a lot more space and a bathroom to yourself. For another $35, they'll turn the air-conditioning on in your room (other wise use the fans). The accommodations are unintentionally rugged, the walls too thin to sleep past 10 AM. But Playa Suave's owners are friendly and reliable, and you're only a short cab ride from all the action. Remember, though, that this is a tiny operation, so there isn't always someone manning the front desk.

If you plan on staying out late, make sure there will be someone awake to let you past the gate when you return. **Pros:** Close to beach and zócalo. **Cons:** Old bed sheets, poorly lighted rooms. ⌷*Costera Miguel Alemán 253, Playa Hamacas* ☎*744/485–1256* ⌷*11 rooms* ⌷*In-room: No a/c, no phone, no TV.* ⌷*No credit cards.*

OLD ACAPULCO

Before the explosion in popularity of jet travel in the late 1960s, the resort areas of Old Acapulco (the Centro, La Quebrada, and the Peninsula de las Playas) were Acapulco. This area still seems to belong to another time, and its ambience is charmingly one of faded elegance. The old grand hotels are cheaper than those outside of town and on the Costera, while the Centro offers accommodation to the traveler on the tightest of budgets.

■TIP→**Old Acapulco is where to find budget hotels and restaurants.**

\$\$\$ ⌷**Alba Suites.** Popular with families, this all-white, all-suites hotel comprises seven low-rise buildings—most four or five stories—with units sleeping four, six, or eight. All have terraces and some also have kitchenettes, which you can stock at the on-site grocery store. There's a cable car to the hotel's beach club, which is on the bay and next to the Club de Yates and its 330-foot-long toboggan run. If you want to play close to your room, there are five pools and a long, curvy water slide. **Pros:** Considerate service, cable car to beach club. **Cons:** Kids are noisy as they play in the pool, decor is basic. ⌷*Grand Via Tropical 35, Caleta* ☎*744/483–0073, 877/428–1327 in Canada* ⌷*www.alba-suites.com.mx* ⌷*300 suites* ⌷*In-room: Kitchen (some), refrigerator. In-hotel: Restaurant, bar, 5 pools, laundry service.* ⌷*AE, MC, V* ⌷*EP.*

\$\$–\$\$\$ ⌷**El Mirador.** Another '50s Hollywood hangout, El Mirador exudes nostalgia, with white walls, red-tile roofs, and hand-carved Mexican furnishings. It's on a hill with great views of Bahía de Acapulco and La Quebrada, where the cliff divers perform. One of the pools is a saltwater one, set naturally between the La Quebrada cliffs. Many suites have refrigerators, hot tubs, and ocean vistas. **Pros:** Wonderful views. **Cons:** Food is inconsistent and there's the sense that its "heyday" has passed. ⌷*Av. Quebrada 74, Old Acapulco* ☎*744/483–1155, 866/765–0608 in U.S.* ⌷*www.hotelelmiradora*

capulco.com.mx ⤶133 rooms, 9 suites ⚴In-room: Refrigerator (some). In-hotel: 2 restaurants, bar, 5 pools, no elevator, children's programs (ages 3–12), laundry service, parking (no fee). ▤AE, MC, V†◎EP .

$–$$$ ▦**Etel Suites.** On Cerro Pinzona (Pinzona Hill), a five-minute walk from La Quebrada, the Etel has outstanding views of Bahía de Acapulco and spacious rooms with sturdy cedar furniture. All accommodations sleep three, and you can rent a full kitchen and dining room to turn your room into a suite. One studio has a kitchenette. There's a garden on the roof and a children's play area by the pool. The owner, gracious Señora Etel Alvarez, is the great-grandniece of John Augustus Sutter, whose mine launched the California Gold Rush of 1849. **Pros:** Near the cliff divers, reasonably priced, wonderful owner. **Cons:** Accommodations are basic. ✉*Av. Pinzona 92, Old Acapulco* ☎744/482–2240⤶12 rooms ⚴In-room: Kitchen (some). In-hotel: Pool, no elevator. ▤MC, V ◎EP .

$$ ▦**Boca Chica.** An Old Acapulco mainstay, right down to its antique telephone switchboard, Boca Chica is a few steps from a swimming cove, and the open-air lobby has lovely views of Bahía de Caletilla. Rooms are small and clean. There's also a landscaped jungle garden and a pool. The Mexican breakfasts are ample and the restaurant's sushi gets thumbs up. **Pros:** Nice views, well-kept gardens. **Cons:** Rooms could use a little TLC. ✉*Playa Caletilla, across bay from Isla la Roqueta and Mágico Mundo Marino, Old Acapulco* ☎744/483–6741, 800/346–3942 in U.S. ⊕*www. acapulco-bocachica.com* ⤶42 rooms, 3 suites ⚴In-hotel: Restaurant, bar, pool, beachfront, diving, water sports, no elevator, laundry service, parking (no fee). ▤MC, V ◎BP .

$–$$ ▦**Los Flamingos.** This hot-pink, cliff-side hotel was a favorite
★   hangout of co-owners John Wayne and Johnny ("Tarzan") Weissmuller. A young busboy at the hotel in those days, Adolfo Santiago, is now the owner. He plays an amazing guitar and, if in the mood, will share some good stories. Today Los Flamingos draws an international clientele for its fine views and its *coco locos*, tequila drinks served in a green coconut. Rooms have bright pink walls and spartan, shower-only baths. Weissmuller liked to stay in the circular two-bedroom master suite. The hotel provides free transportation to the beach and downtown. **Pros:** History is intriguing, epic views. **Cons:** A little wear and tear in

rooms, bathrooms need updating. ⊠*Av. López Mateos, Fracc. las Playas, Old Acapulco* ☎744/482–0690 ⊕*www. hotellosflamingos.com* ⚲*46 rooms, 2 suites* ⚿*In-room: No a/c (some). In-hotel: Restaurant, bar, pool, no elevator, laundry service, parking (no fee)* ⊟*AE, MC, V.*

¢ ⚏**Casa de Huespedes Sutter.** These, the very cheapest accommodations in all of Acapulco, are surprisingly decent. The clean courtyard hotel, though nothing exciting, is old enough to have the atmosphere of the 1950s resort. The friendly proprietor is happy to give you loads of information about visiting the city, and the place is just steps from the malecón and the Centro's best restaurants. A shaded terrace under a long clothesline makes for a comfortable perch on hot afternoons. The rooms are spartan but well-maintained, and the views of the surrounding rooftops and crazy streets uphill toward La Quebrada evoke the look of Spanish coastal towns, allowing guests to feel like they're in Europe while slumming it in Acapulco. **Pros:** Comfortable beds, clean rooms and public areas, convenient location. **Cons:** No kitchen for guests; since ground-floor rooms on the courtyard have their doors all in a line, they lack a bit of privacy. ⊠*Calle Benito Juàrez 12, Centro* ☎744/422–2396 ⚲*26 rooms* ⚿*In-room: Safe, no phone, no TV. In-hotel: No elevator.* ⊟*No credit cards.*

¢ ⚏**Hotel Alameda.** Overlooking the leafy zócalo, what looks like a dilapidated tenement is really a clean, well-appointed, and exceedingly comfortable budget hotel that might be Acapulco's best-kept secret. The cheapest Internet in town is downstairs in the same building (as is the Centro's best café) and a rooftop deck overlooks a fountain and gazebo in the square and a section of the harbor and hills around the bay. A mural in the deck area shows the site in 1757, when a log cabin hugged the shore; 1857, when it was an elegant Spanish house, and 1957, Old Acapulco's heyday, when the hotel opened. **Pros:** Unbeatable in-city location, comfortable beds, and spacious bathrooms. **Cons:** Noise goes on until midnight on the zócalo, fans instead of a/c in rooms and barred windows contribute to the exterior's "ruined" look. ⊠*Calle Benito Juàrez 2, Centro* ☎744/482–8423 ⚲*21 rooms* ⚿*In-room: No a/c, no phone, no TV. In-hotel: No elevator.* ⊟*No credit cards.*

¢ ⚏**Misión.** Two minutes from the zócalo, this charming, colonial-style hotel surrounds a greenery-rich courtyard with an outdoor eating area that's open only for breakfast.

Rooms are small and by no means fancy, with painted brick walls, tile floors, wrought-iron beds, and ceiling fans. Every room has a shower, and there's plenty of hot water. The best rooms are on the second and third floors, as you can open the windows and fully appreciate the view; the top-floor room is large but hot in the daytime. **Pros:** Artistic touches, quaint feel, gorgeous building. **Cons:** Tiny rooms, no lunch or dinner. In spring, huge mangoes drop from the 60-foot tree in the courtyard all night, crashing loudly onto the roof. ⊠*Calle Felipe Valle 12, Downtown* ☎744/482–3643 ⤳*20 rooms* ⚿*In-room: No a/c, no phone, no TV. In-hotel: No elevator.* ⊟*No credit cards*☉*EP.*

ACAPULCO DIAMANTE

Most of the newer, more expensive resorts are in Acapulco Diamante and Playa Revolcadero. These resorts are designed to keep you captive by offering the total vacation experience (except for all-inclusive packages), including restaurants, clubs, spas, expansive grounds, beautiful beaches, and in some cases, golf courses. Acapulco proper is a $15 taxi ride away.

$$$$ 🖭**Camino Real Acapulco Diamante.** This stunning hotel is at
★ the foot of a lush hill on exclusive Playa Pichilingue, far from the madding crowd. All rooms are done in pastels and have tile floors, luxurious baths, and up-to-date amenities such as laptop-size safes outfitted with chargers; all rooms also have balconies or terraces with a view of peaceful Puerto Marqués bay. Eleven extra-spacious club rooms have their own concierge and extra amenities. **Pros:** Good-size rooms, nice views. **Cons:** Pool can get busy, little to do within walking distance. ⊠*Calle Baja Catita off Carretera Escénica at Km 14, Acapulco Diamante* ☎744/435–1010, *800/722–6466 in U.S.* ⊕*www.caminoreal.com/acapulco* ⤳*146 rooms, 11 suites* ⚿*In-room: Safe, refrigerator, Wi-Fi. In-hotel: 3 restaurants, room service, bars, pools, gym, spa, beachfront, water sports, concierge, children's programs (ages 5–15), laundry service, no-smoking rooms, Internet.* ⊟*AE, DC, MC, V*☉*EP.*

$$$$ 🖭**Quinta Real.** A member of Mexico's most prestigious hotel
★ chain, this low-slung hillside resort overlooks the sea, about a 15-minute drive from downtown. The 74 suites have balconies, Mexican-made hardwood furniture, and closet door handles shaped like iguanas—a signature motif. Six suites have private hot tubs and small pools on their balconies.

Pros: Nice facilities, great "world music" in the common areas. **Cons:** Not much to do at night, service is not up to snuff for the price you pay. ⊠*Paseo de la Quinta Lote 6, Acapulco Diamante, Real Diamante* ☎744/469–1500, 866/621–9288 *in U.S.* ⊕*www.quintareal.com* ⇥*74 suites* ⌂*In-hotel: Restaurant, room service, bar, pools, gym, spa, beachfront, water sports, concierge, laundry service, public Wi-Fi.* ⊟*AE, MC, V* ⓘ*EP.*

★ **Fodor's**Choice ⊠ **Fairmont Acapulco Princess.** The three-tower
$$$–$$$$ Princess lures the rich and famous (Howard Hughes once hid away in a suite here). Near the reception desk, fantastic ponds with waterfalls and a slatted bridge hint at the luxury throughout. Large, airy rooms have cane furniture, marble floors, and wireless Internet access. You can dine in six excellent restaurants, then burn off the calories in a match at the tennis center, which is large enough to host the Mexican Open every year. Less taxing is the internationally rated golf course. The superb Willow Stream spa, open to guests and nonguests, has aromatherapy, thalassotherapy, and body wraps, plus a fitness center, Swiss showers, a hair salon, and a Jacuzzi. A shuttle runs frequently to the adjacent Pierre Marqués, where all facilities are also available. **Pros:** Elaborate pools, nice golf course. **Cons:** Caters to conventions, so can be crowded, beach can get busy. ⊠*Playa Revolcadero, Granjas del Marqués* ⌖*A. P. 135, 39907* ☎744/469–1000, 800/441–1414 *in U.S., 01800/090–9900 in Mexico* ⊕*www.fairmont.com* ⇥*927 rooms, 92 suites* ⌂*In-room: Safe, dial-up, Ethernet. In-hotel: 7 restaurants, room service, bars, golf course, tennis courts, pools, gym, spa, beachfront, water sports, concierge, children's programs (ages 3–12), laundry service.* ⊟*AE, DC, MC, V* ⓘ*BP, EP* .

WHEN TO RENT. If you're traveling in a group of four or more couples, renting a villa can be a fun and reasonably priced option for your Acapulco vacation. The best rentals are perched up in the hills of Las Brisas, and generally run from $350 a day for a four-bedroom during low season, to about $2,000 a day for an extravagant 10-bedroom over Christmas vacation. A Web site like ⊕*www.villasinacapulco.com* is an excellent place to start your search. Prime rental properties go quickly, so plan your stay no less than four weeks in advance.

★ Fodor'sChoice ⚏ **Fairmont Pierre Marqués.** This boutique-style
$$$–$$$$ hotel was built by J. Paul Getty in 1958 as a personal
retreat. Longtime employees say that he never used it,
instead making it available to his friends before eventually
turning it into a hotel. After a multimillion-dollar renova-
tion in 2004, the Pierre Marqués is still one of Mexico's
finest properties. The hotel offers the serenity and sophis-
tication of a private hacienda but with the first-class ser-
vices and amenities of an international resort, including a
meandering pool overlooking the ocean. You can stay in a
room or suite in the tower building or in one of the ultra-
luxe villas or bungalows, which have private plunge pools.
A shuttle runs frequently to the adjacent Princess, where
you can use all facilities. **Pros:** High-quality golf course,
well-kept grounds. **Cons:** Food is pricey, can't get anywhere
without a taxi. ⊠*Playa Revolcadero, Granjas del Marqués
⑉A.P. 1351, 39907 ☎744/466–1000, 800/441–1414 in
U.S., 01800/090–9900 in Mexico ⊕www.fairmont.com
⤳220 rooms, 74 executive premier rooms, 25 suites, 10
villas, 4 bungalows ⚘In-room: Safe, refrigerator (some),
dial-up, Ethernet. In-hotel: 2 restaurants, room service,
bar, golf course, tennis courts, pools, beachfront, concierge,
children's programs (ages 3–12), laundry service, public
Wi-Fi.* ▤*AE, DC, MC, V* ⦿*BP, EP.*

$$ ⚏ **Hotel Terrazas.** Spectacularly set along the hillside at the
far end of Playa Puerto Marqués, this spacious and friendly
hotel takes full advantage of its scenic locale. A perfect
parallelogram swimming pool occupies the center of the
middle deck, tucked under a comfortable restaurant area
with one of the best natural views in town. Playa Revolcadero is 10 minutes away along an adjacent back road,
but there isn't much reason to go: the scenery and all the
swimming you might want are here (the clean and cheer-
ful rooms could use more amenities, though). Discounts
are available for groups; prices are 30% higher during
December and Easter week. **Pros:** Just gorgeous, inside
and out, and directly across from one of Acapulco's best
swimming beaches. **Cons:** The lack of phones is intentional,
but a little bit of a chafe. The neighborhood is somewhat
seedy and abandoned after dark. ⊠*Managua 100, Puerto
Marqués ☎744/466–0081 ⤳72 rooms ⚘In-room: No
a/c (some), no phones, refrigerator (some), no TV (some).
In-hotel: Restaurant, bar, pool, laundry service, no elevator.* ▤*AE, MC, V.*

¢–$ ⓘ**Hostal Kingdom.** Inland at a former training camp for Olympic athletes, and the very opposite of what the word "hostel" usually suggests, this spacious campus includes a tennis court, running track, soccer field, and Olympic-size swimming pool. The dormitories have four bunk beds to a room, with separate and shared (but enormous) bathrooms and showers. The beach at Puerto Marqués is about a half-mile away, and the frequent buses into town take about 30 minutes. A shared kitchen is available, and the five-person suites have their own kitchens. The place is usually nearly empty, but is a good option for budget travelers seeking exercise, peace, and quiet. **Pros:** Friendly staff, great sports facilities and quiet public areas. **Cons:** Far from things, near a peripheral highway bridge. ⊠*Glorieta Puerto Marqués 104, Glorieta Puerto Marqués* ☎*744/466–4152* ⇩*3 4-bed dorms, 5 suites, 2 single bungalows* ⓘ*In-room: No phone, no TV, kitchens (some), Wi-Fi. In-hotel: Tennis court, pool, public Wi-Fi, no elevator.* ⊟*No credit cards.*

¢–$ ⓘ**Hotel Gabachines.** An unusual combination of hotel and youth hostel, this is the only low-price hotel in Acapulco directly across from a beach (and that beach is Puerto Marqués, the loveliest and cleanest swimming beach in the area).The eight rooms are each equipped with three beds: solo travelers may find themselves joined in their rooms by other guests, though two can rent a room for themselves. There's an Internet café and a storage safe in the lobby, and a stretch of cheap beachfront restaurants across the street. The area is a humble and friendly neighborhood for Mexicans seeking a beach getaway and often feels like a small coastal village, but is eerily abandoned at night except for a few small grocery stores. **Pros:** Friendly vibe, a gathering place for interesting international backpackers. **Cons:** No guarantee for singles of a private room without paying the cost of three, and the three-story building has no elevator. ⊠*Av. Costera Miguel Alemàn s/n, Playa Puerto Marqués* ☎*744/433–7003* ⇩*8 dorm rooms* ⓘ*In-room: No phone. In-hotel: No elevator, public Internet.* ⊟*No credit cards.*

LAS BRISAS

$$$$ ⓘ**Las Brisas.** Perhaps Acapulco's signature resort, this hilltop haven is particularly popular with honeymooners. (The company motto is actually "Where children are seldom seen, but often created.") There are a variety of quarters, from one-bedroom units to deluxe private casitas complete with small private pools. Room interiors are a little dated, but nobody seems to mind because of the enchanting bay views. Since the property is spread out (all rooms are at ground level), transportation is by pink-and-white Jeeps. The hotel also provides transportation to its private beach club, five minutes away. A continental breakfast is delivered to your room each morning. **Pros:** Astounding views from almost everywhere, gracious service. **Cons:** Room interiors dated, wait for Jeeps can be 20 minutes, pricey for what you get. ⊠*Carretera Escénica Clemente Mejía 5255, Las Brisas* ☎744/469–6900, 888/559–4329 in U.S. and Canada ⊕*www.brisas.com.mx* ⊅*300 units* ⚑*In-room: Wi-Fi. In-hotel: 2 restaurants, bars, tennis courts, 3 pools, water sports, concierge, laundry service, public Wi-Fi, no elevator.* ⊟*MC, V* ⓘⓞⒾ*CP.*

BARRA VIEJA

Just east of Acapulco Diamante and the airport but barely touched by the gradual sprawl of development, Barra Vieja holds a long strand of poor houses and shack restaurants. The area's restaurants are singularly famous for their specialty, pescado à la talla, a smokey, buttery fish filet cooked in mayonnaise. But the town's other claim to fame is that it hosts what are probably the best two hotels in Acapulco.

★ **Fodor'sChoice** ⌂**Casa Yal'ma Ka'an.** This might be the most un-
$$$$ Acapulqueño of Acapulco hotels: its garden holds a perfect circle of Polynesian-style, porch-fronted cedar cabins on flood stilts. Inside the cabins are warmly decorated and cleaner than clean. The delightful boutique hotel's grounds include a pool, restaurant, temezcal (a Mayan-style sweat lodge), and firepit and opens onto a magnificent, deserted strand of white beach. Honeymooners and those whose only aim is to unwind might still be tempted by some healthy stimulation: Indian ritual sweats, yoga classes, Jacuzzi soaks, and massage. The beach bar is open for guests only on weekends. **Pros:** The staff helps plan weddings, and there are beds around the pool. **Cons:** Silence is broken by jets using the nearby airport; the ocean currents are dangerous. ⊠*Carretera Barra Vieja, Km 29.5, Col. Ejido El Podrodido* ☎744/444–6389 ⊕*www.casayalmakaan.com* ⊅*7 cabins* ⚑*In-room: Safe. In-hotel: restaurant, bar, pool, gym, beachfront, no kids under 18.* ⊟*D, MC, V.*

$$$$ ⌂**Villas San Vicente.** Phenomenal is the word for this palm-shaded boutique hotel that resembles a world leader's private beach compound: five individual two-story '60s modernist villas (sleeping six) are separated by a generous expanse of immaculate lawn and face an incredibly scenic (but virtually unswimmable) stretch of wide, sandy beach. The eccentric centerpiece is a 60-foot lighthouse incongruously, which is its own three-story minisuite with a bedroom at the top. Villa interiors have an Italian flair: red drapes, white walls, black fixtures, and fully modern kitchens. The property runs almost like a condo development; not many services are offered. Weddings are frequently held here, and it's easy to see why. A lovelier and more elite setting is virtually impossible to imagine. Deals are available in the off-season. **Pros:** Each villa has its own pool, full kitchen, and TV/DVD. **Cons:** No restaurant, the nearest one is a five-minute drive away, and with all the other luxuries, why no big-screen TVs? ✉ *Carretera Barra Vieja, Km 17.5, Col. Bonfil* ☎ *744/485–6846 or 744/486–4037* ⊕ *www.villassanvicente.com.mx* ➭ *5 villas* ⚭ *In-room: Kitchen, DVD, Wi-Fi. In-hotel: Pool, beachfront.* ▤ *AE, MC, V.*

MOSQUITOS. The pesky little buggers aren't nearly as bad in Acapulco as in most areas along the coast, but persons who attract the insects (through their blood chemistry) should bring repellent, or buy the inexpensive and effective Autan brand of Mexican bug repellent on arrival. In outlying areas, windows have screens or beds have soft mesh mosquito nets that can be taken down at night, when mosquitoes appear. They fly about 12 feet above the ground and find their victims by tracing the updraft of their body heat, so plug any net holes with tissue paper, shut the flap, and unless the net hangs to the floor, tuck it in under the mattress and don't let the material lie directly on your skin.

PIE DE LA CUESTA

To Whom It May Concern: the west of town is the laid-back beach settlement of Pie de la Cuesta, home to low- and mid-price small hotels, usually family-run and on the beach, as well as some more luxurious options. If you stay here, you'll get a good taste of Mexican beach-village life.

$$$$ ▦ **Parador del Sol.** Germans and Canadians favor this low-key, all-inclusive resort's white villas scattered throughout gardens along both the lagoon and the Pacific Ocean sides of Carretera Pie de la Cuesta. The ocean is particularly dramatic here, with towering waves. The spacious rooms

have tile floors and fan-cooled terraces with hammocks. In addition to all meals, comprising Guerrero specialties served buffet-style, including red snapper and tamales, rates include the occasional on-site music and dance performance, aerobics classes, tennis, and nonmotorized water sports. Motorized water sports cost extra. **Pros:** Peaceful, beautiful beach. **Cons:** A trek to downtown by car, rough ocean so swimming is limited, pricey for what you get. ⊠*Carretera Pie de la Cuesta–Barra de Coyuca, Km 5, Pie de la Cuesta* ☝*A.P. 1070 39300* ☎*744/444–4050* ⊕*www. paradordelsol.com.mx* ⇘*150 rooms* ☝*In-hotel: Restaurant, bars, tennis courts, pools, gym, water sports, no elevator, laundry service, parking (no fee).* ⊟*MC, V* ⧦*AI* .

$$–$$$ ⊞**Hotel Casa Blanca.** Opening onto a wide beach, this sunny, white-stucco boutique retreat has gorgeously furnished guestrooms. Suites face the water on both sides and the courtyard holds the rooms that are cheaper and don't have hot water. The attached French restaurant is excellent. A little pool cozies up to a shady bar and restaurant area, and scattered palm trees complete the Moorish vibe. Long palm-frond shelters stand along the beach, and guests move freely between the water, the shelters and the courtyard, having the time of their lives. **Pros:** Attention to detail in the architecture and room decor, beach has a lifeguard and snack cart in the afternoon. **Cons:** The staff is a little scattered, and the courtyard becomes a small wind tunnel when the breeze kicks in. ⊠*Playa del Sol 370, Pie de la Cuesta* ☎*744/460–0324 or 744/460–4028* ⇗casablanca@ prodigy.net.mx ⇘*8 rooms, 6 suites* ☝*In-room: No phones, no TV (some), Wi-Fi (some). In-hotel: Restaurant, bar, pool, public Wi-Fi.* ⊟*No credit cards.*

★ Fodor'sChoice ⊞**Hacienda Vayma.** White-stucco bungalows **$–$$$** named for musicians and painters overlook the beach or interior courtyards. The sparse, contemporary rooms accommodate two, three, or five people. The bathrooms are tiny, however, and have no hot water. If you can opt for one of the suites, which have plunge pools, air-conditioning, and terraces, you'll be a lot more comfortable. An excellent outdoor restaurant draws diners from miles around, and on weekends the hotel fills with an interesting array of guests, such as embassy personnel from Mexico City. **Pros:** Animals allowed, some rooms have canopied beds. **Cons:** No credit cards accepted. ⊠*Av. Base Aerea Militar 378, Pie de la Cuesta* ☎*744/460–5260* ⊕*www.vayma. com.mx* ⇘*20 rooms, 4 suites* ☝*In-room: no a/c (some),* *no phone. In-hotel: Restaurant, bar, pool, spa, beachfront, water sports, no elevator, laundry service, parking (no fee), some pets allowed.* ▭ *No credit cards* ⏹ *EP.*

$-$$ ⬚**Villas Ukae Kim.** You can't miss this colorful, rustic, sea-side lodge. The large rooms are painted in bright Mexican hues, and all have terraces and mosquito nets slung over double beds; the honeymoon suite has a private hot tub. **Pros:** Artistic touches. **Cons:** No credit cards accepted. ✉ *Av. Fuerza Aereo Mexicana 356, Pie de la Cuesta* ☎ */44/440–0486* ⬚ *21 rooms, 1 suite* ⬚ *In-room: No a/c (some), no phone, no TV (some). In-hotel: Restaurant, bar, pool, beachfront, water sports, no elevator, laundry service, parking (no fee).* ▭ *No credit cards* ⏹ *EP .*

Where to Eat

WORD OF MOUTH

"The one thing that Acapulco has going for [it] is the variety of restaurants. There are so many great restaurants."

—acame

By Grand
Cogswell
&
Jonathan
J. Levin

ACAPULCO DEVELOPED AS A TOURIST TOWN CATERING TO THOSE ESCAPING MEXICO CITY, so the local cuisine takes its cues from the tastes of the capitol. Once the allure of Acapulco caught the attention of international travelers, restaurants began broadening their scope to please their palates above all else. Beef is shipped from Sonora and Chihuahua (and New Zealand) to be handled in the Continental manner by French-trained chefs, and local seafood is well-handled in a popular French-Asian fusion style, occasionally straying closer to local methods of preparation. Unfortunately, the places that market themselves as pure Japanese or Chinese restaurants tend to fall flat on their faces. Sampling the region's fine seafood is requisite to experiencing the city, and the best restaurants in town often specialize in the local catches.

You could dine on a different cuisine every night of the week, whether you opt for a small, authentic *loncheria* (small, family-run café) serving regional favorites or a fine-dining establishment requiring advance reservations. In another nod to the European and North American tourist influx, restaurants make it their practice to serve large evening meals, which runs counter to the national habit.

All of the restaurants on the Costera Miguel Alemán are slightly over-priced. The best of them embrace local tradition, at least to a certain extent. Mexican-style seafood restaurants are always a good bet, as are the few restaurants that fuse local cuisine with Thai or Mediterranean flavors. You'll find dozens of beachside eateries with palapa roofs, as well as wildly decorated rib and hamburger joints full of people of all ages who enjoy a casual, sometimes raucous, time.

A few excellent fine restaurants on the Carretera Escénica and in Pie de la Cuesta offer sophisticated cuisine that draws its influences from abroad, while reinterpreting domestic specialties like pescado à la talla—fish cooked in a wood oven with a chile adobo (a kind of mayonnaise marinade)—which is equally well enjoyed in beach shacks in Pie de la Cuesta and the dish's home turf, Barra Vieja, where you can take a boat through the mangroves to one of many dining huts. If you're in search of cheap eats, wander inland where you'll rub shoulders with locals. In Old Acapulco, (near the zócalo, the main plaza, at La Quebrada and on the Peninsula de las Playas) restaurants cater to the tastes of their mostly Mexican clientele and offer more traditional fare.

If it's luxury you're after, take a cab out to Las Brisas, the romantic hillside neighborhood where investors have built some of the area's best new restaurants. To ensure seating in Acapulco's most exclusive dining rooms, it's often necessary to make reservations a few days in advance.

As for eating on the go, there's also a great antojito (tacos, sopes, quesadillas) tradition here. In general, there's no reason not to trust the street food. During the day, women will walk around hawking spicy homemade tamales on the sidewalk. In Acapulco they're usually moister from being cooked in banana leaves, unlike in other regions where they're wrapped in cornhusks.

ABOUT THE RESTAURANTS

Expect to pay $25 or more for a main course at the best restaurants in town, where views of the ocean are often fantastic. Ties and jackets are out of place, but so are shorts and jeans, except for in the inexpensive places. Unless stated otherwise, all restaurants are open daily for lunch and dinner; dinner-only places open around 6:30 or 7. Acapulqueños rarely go out for dinner before 8 pm, and club-bound young people often eat even later.

Outside the city in Pie de la Cuesta and Barra Vieja, even the finest restaurant may not accept credit cards. Closer in, on the Costera, Carretera Escènica, and in the hotel restaurants of Acapulco Diamante, credit cards are accepted universally. ■TIP➔ **Mexicans always take their time at restaurants, and waiters will never bring your check until you ask for it. So follow some classic advice—"When in Rome, do as the Romans do"—and allow yourself an extra 20 or 30 minutes to chat with your company at the table.**

When aiming for a simple, budget meal, note that the less rigorously an establishment tries to attract tourists (i.e., with English-language signs, A-frames on the sidewalk, hawkers) the better the food is: places that count on return business of locals are usually the best.

Early risers are not rewarded with breakfast here—most restaurants don't serve it until 9 am so stock up on some groceries to tide you over. The biggest dining pitfall for tourists is food-borne illness. Avoid streetside juices, fruit cocktails, and cupped flan. Long-term visitors will have to get sick in order to develop immunity, so in that case, dig in. Most restaurants purify their drinking and cooking water, but if you don't want to take any risks, ask for bottled drinking water.

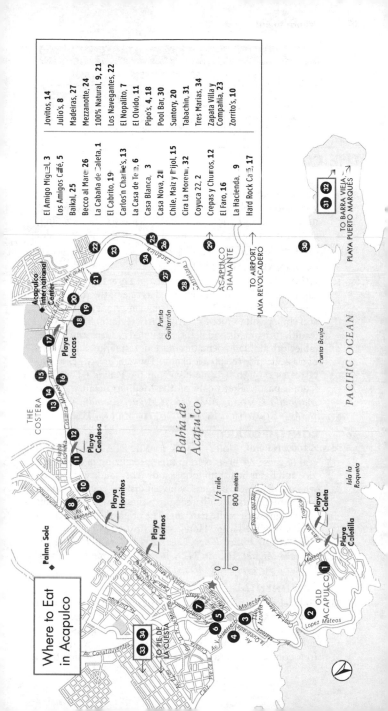

Where to Eat in Acapulco

El Amigo Miguel, **3**
Los Amigos Café, **5**
Baikal, **25**
Becco al Mare **26**
La Cabaña de Caleta, **1**
El Cabrito, **19**
Carlos'n Charlie's, **13**
La Casa de Tere, **6**
Casa Blanca, **3**
Casa Nova, **28**
Chile, Maiz y Frijol, **15**
Cira La Morena, **32**
Coyuca 22, **2**
Crepas y Churros, **12**
El Faro, **16**
La Hacienda, **9**
Hard Rock Cafe, **17**

Jovito's, **14**
Julio's, **8**
Madeiras, **27**
Mezzanotte, **24**
100% Natural, **9, 21**
Los Navegantes, **22**
El Nopalito, **7**
El Olvido, **11**
Pipo's, **4, 18**
Pool Bar, **30**
Suntory, **20**
Tabachin, **31**
Tres Marias, **34**
Zapata Villa y
Compañia, **23**
Zorrito's, **10**

PACIFIC OCEAN

Bahía de Acapulco

ACAPULCO DIAMANTE

TO AIRPORT, PLAYA REVOLCADERO

TO BARRA VIEJA, PLAYA PUERTO MARQUÉS →

THE COSTERA

Acapulco International Center

Playa Icacos

Playa Condesa

Playa Hornitos

Playa Hornos

Palma Sola

OLD ACAPULCO

Playa Caleta

Playa Caletilla

Isla la Roqueta

Punta Guitarrón

Punta Bruja

TO PIE DE LA CUESTA

0   1/2 mile
0   800 meters

WHAT IT COSTS IN DOLLARS				
¢	$	$$	$$$	$$$$
under $5	$5–$10	$10–$15	$15–$25	over $25

Restaurant prices are for a main course excluding tax and tip.

THE COSTERA

Loud music blares from many restaurants along the Costera, especially those facing Playa Condesa, and proprietors will aggressively try to hustle you inside with offers of drink specials. If you're looking for a more sedate evening, avoid this area or decide in advance where to dine and head straight there.

INTERNATIONAL/ECLECTIC

$$$–$$$$ ✕ **El Olvido.** With an eclectic menu and a great bayside location, El Olvido is well established as one of the top restaurants on the Costera. Dishes like quail in a honey, pineapple, and chile pasilla sauce expertly marry regional flavors with traditions from abroad. Palm tree–lined gardens and white-tablecloth ambience lend this outdoor restaurant an element of class, despite the plastic chairs. The rich, creamy tiramisu tastes as though it came not from the Pacific Coast, but from a pastry chef's café on the Mediterranean. ⊠ *Plaza Maribella Costera, Av. Costera Miguel Alemán, Costera* ☎ *744/481–0203* ♣ *Reservations essential* ⊟ *MC, V*

CONTEMPORARY

¢–$ ✕ **100% Natural.** Along the Costera Miguel Alemán are several of these 24-hour restaurants specializing in quick service and light, healthful food: sandwiches made with whole wheat bread, soy burgers, chicken dishes, yogurt shakes, and fruit salads. You'll recognize these eateries by their green signs with white lettering. The original—and best—is across from the Grand Hotel. ⊠ *Av. Costera Miguel Alemán 234, near Acapulco Plaza, Costera* ☎ *744/485–3982* ⊠ *Av. Costera Miguel Alemán 3126, in front of Hotel La Palapa, Costera* ☎ *744/484–8440* ⊟ *DC, MC, V*

CONTINENTAL

$$$–$$$$ ✕ **Madeiras.** All tables at this elegant restaurant have views
★ of the bay, and the dishes and flatware were created by Taxco silversmiths. In the bar-reception area, groovy glass coffee tables rest on carved wooden animals. Dinner is a four-course, prix-fixe meal, and there are 15 menus from

which to choose. Specialties include tasty chilled soups and red snapper baked in sea salt (a Spanish dish); there are also steak choices, lobster tail, chicken, and pork. ✉*Carretera Escénica 33-Bis, just past La Vista shopping center, Costera* ☎744/446–5636 ⊕*www.modernmexican.com* ⌂*Reservations essential* ▤*AE, MC, V* ⊗*No lunch*

JAPANESE

$$$–$$$$ ✕**Suntory.** You can dine in the delightful Asian-style garden or in an air conditioned room. Suntory is one of Acapulco's few Japanese restaurants and one of the few deluxe places that's open for lunch. Many diners opt for the *teppanyaki* (thin slices of beef and vegetables seared on a hot grill), prepared at your table by skilled chefs. Rib eye and seafood are also on the menu, but not sushi. ✉*Av. Costera Miguel Alemán 36, across from La Palapa hotel, Costera* ☎744/484–8088 ▤*AE, MC, V.*

SEAFOOD

$$–$$$$ ✕**Pipo's.** On a rather quiet stretch of the Costera, this old,
★ family-run restaurant doesn't have an especially interesting view, but locals come here for the fresh fish, good service, and reasonable prices for most dishes. Try the huachinango veracruzano (red snapper baked with tomatoes, peppers, onion, and olives) or the fillet of fish in mojo de ajo (garlic butter). The original location downtown is also popular with locals. ✉ *Av. Costera Miguel Alemán and Nao Victoria, across from Acapulco International Center, Costera* ☎744/484–0165 ✉*Calle Almirante Bretón 3 Old Acapulco* ☎/44/482–2237 ▤*AE, MC, V*

$–$$$$ ✕**Los Navegantes.** A line often goes out the door at this popular seafood restaurant on the second floor of El Tropicano Hotel. If you get a table by the window, you'll have views of the bustling Costera below. Most dishes, including the popular *filete habañero* (tilapia bathed in a creamy chili sauce), come accompanied with beans or rice and handmade tortillas. ✉*Costera Miguel Alemán 20, Local A, Costera* ☎744/484–2101 ▤*AE, MC, V.*

$–$$$ ✕**El Amigo Miguel.** The first place a local will probably recommend for good, reasonably priced seafood on the beach is El Amigo Miguel, which lies between the "Golden Zone" western side of the Costera and Old Acapulco. With the dining room frequently bustling, it may be tempting to move on to one of the nearby seafood joints, but there are good reasons why locals flock here and its neighbors are next to empty: the service is far superior, and the seafood is as fresh as you could hope for. ⊠ *Av. Costera Miguel Alemán s/n, Costera* ☎*744/483–6981* ▤*AE, MC, V.*

$–$$ ✕**Julio's.** The locals rave about Julio's, where they know
★ they'll get a great variety of fresh seafood at an affordable price. There's nothing fancy here except the fresh authentic Mexican dishes served by friendly folks. Try the shrimp tacos or the barbecued whole fish, preceded by a large seafood cocktail. A fish fillet dinner costs about $7. Most tourists haven't found this place yet, so for a great cultural and dining experience that won't empty your wallet, this is the place. ⊠*Cristóbal Colón 56, Costera* ☎*744/485–3289* ▤*MC, V*

MEXICAN

$$–$$$ ✕**Zapata, Villa y Compañia.** The music and the food are strictly local, and the memorabilia recall the Mexican Revolution— guns, hats, and photographs of Pancho Villa. Often the evening's highlight is a visit from a sombrero-wearing baby burro, so be sure to bring your camera. The menu includes the ever-popular fajitas, tacos, and grilled meats. ⊠*Hyatt Regency Acapulco, Av. Costera Miguel Alemán 1, Costera* ☎*744/469–1234* ▤*AE, DC, MC, V* ⊘*No lunch.*

> **WORD OF MOUTH.** "For just good Mexican food, don't miss El Cabrito on the Costera, near the CiCi water park. Outstanding moles. Also, great ceviche and the specialty is cabrito, baby goat, though that isn't my kind of thing. Very informal; no air conditioning." –tengohambre

$–$$ ✕**El Cabrito.** As the name implies, young goat—served char-coal-grilled—is a specialty of this restaurant, open since 1963. You can also choose from among such truly Mexican dishes as chicken in *mole* (spicy chocolate-chili sauce); shrimp in tequila; and jerky with egg, fish, and seafood. Wash it down with a cold beer or glass of wine. ⊠*Av. Costera Miguel Alemán 1480, between CiCi and Centro Internacional, Costera* ☎*744/484–7711* ▤*MC, V*

$–$$ ✕**La Casa de Tere.** Hidden in a shopping district downtown (signs point the way), this spotless open-air eatery with pink walls is in a league of its own—expect beer-hall tables and chairs, colorful Mexican decorations, and photos of Acapulco of yore. The varied menu includes outstanding *sopa de tortilla* (tortilla soup), chicken mole, and flan. ⊠*Calle Alonso Martín 1721, 2 blocks from Av. Costera Miguel Alemán, Costera* ☎*744/485–7735* ▤*No credit cards* ⊘*Closed Mon.*

CLOSE UP

Breakfast Deals

There's no excuse for skipping breakfast in Acapulco—there are just too many great restaurants (but note, in this late-night town, they don't open until 9 am). Charming and inexpensive restaurants line the Costera, such as Chile, Maiz y Frijol, where you can get an order of eggs à la mexicana for about US$4. In Acapulco, breakfast is always under $7, and for as little as $3, you can land a big breakfast of eggs, meat, beans, tortillas, juice and/or coffee. This morning meal trade is purely for tourists: Mexicans elsewhere tend to eat light in the morning and evening, and take a long lunch into the afternoon.

If breakfast is your main meal of the day, head to the eastern end of the Costera for the Hyatt Regency's vast buffet spread. Sample a little of everything: an omelet, a serving of chilaquiles (be careful, they can weigh you down), or a waffle smothered in maple syrup.

4

$–$$ ✕**Zorrito's.** When Julio Iglesias is in town, he heads to this
★ open-air street-side eatery after the discos close. It's open almost all the time, serving Acapulco's famous green-and-white *pozole* (pork and hominy soup) as well as such steak dishes as *filete tampiqueña* (a strip of tender grilled beef), which comes with tacos, enchiladas, guacamole, and beans. ✉*Av. Costera Miguel Alemán and Calle Anton de Alaminos, next to Banamex, Costera* ☎*744/485–3735* ▭*AE, MC, V* ☾*No lunch Tues.*

¢–$ ✕**Chile, Maiz y Frijol.** If the extravagant buffets and the four-star restaurants of Acapulco get tiresome, slip into this great little place for breakfast, a real Mexican restaurant. The huevos rancheros are perfectly done—not too runny—and buried beneath a pool of salsa. Though the options are fewer, the lunch and dinner menus are equally well-priced. ✉ *Av. Costera Miguel Alemán 116, Costera* ☎*774/481–0300* ▭*No credit cards.*

RICK SAYS. Check out *www.travel-acapulco.com*, a Web site that started as a travelogue by a Texas native named Rick, who moved to Acapulco in early 2003. His reviews, advice, and suggestions for activities are reliable and fun to read.

AMERICAN

$$–$$$ ✕**Hard Rock Cafe.** This link in the international Hard Rock chain is one of Acapulco's most popular spots, among locals as well as visitors. The New York–cut steaks, hamburgers, and brownies, as well as the Southern-style fried chicken and ribs are familiar and satisfying. Taped rock music begins at noon, and a live group starts playing at 10 PM on Thursday, Friday, and Saturday. ⊠*Av. Costera Miguel Alemán 37, Costera* ☎744/484–6680 ⊕*www.hardrock. com* ▤*AE, DC, MC, V*

ITALIAN

$$–$$$ ✕**Mezzanotte.** You may end up dancing with your waiter—perhaps atop a table—on a Friday or Saturday evening; you'll definitely end up mixing with the who's who of Acapulco just about any night of the week. The stylish interior has a large sunken dining area, original sculptures, and huge bay windows looking out to sea. Patrons rave about the fettuccine with smoked salmon in avocado sauce and the charcoal-grilled sea bass with shrimp and artichokes in a citrus sauce. For a light ending to your meal, try the gelato. Music videos are projected on large screens on weekends. ⊠*Carretera Escénica 28, L-2, in La Vista shopping center, Costera* ☎744/446–5727 ▤*AE, MC, V* ⊗*No lunch*

AMERICAN/MEXICAN

$–$$$ ✕**Carlos and Charlie's.** A Mexican institution of sorts, Carlos and Charlie's is best known for its flamboyant interior—a lot of cow imagery, among other miscellany—along with its family friendly atmosphere. Like a T.G.I. Friday's, the restaurant serves variations of Mexican, Italian, and American dishes, none of them capable of wooing food critics. But with employees making balloon animals in the middle of the dining room, it's clear that Carlos and Charlie's is an establishment that charges for good times, not outstanding food. ⊠*Av. Costera Miguel Alemán 112, Costera* ☎744/484–0039 ⊕*www.carlosandcharlies.com* ▤*MC, V*

MEXICAN/SEAFOOD

$–$$$ ✕**Jovitos.** Jovitos's fish and shrimp tacos are arguably the finest in Acapulco, owing as much to the presentation—seafood served in ceramic bowls, with cheese oozing over the edges—as the delicious ingredients, all served in a casual open-air setting. Each dish is served with 12 different salsas, and every one is worth a try. ⊠*Av. Costera Miguel Alemán 108, Costera* ☎744/484–5375 ▤*MC, V.*

$–$$$$ ✕**El Faro.** Classy El Faro resembles a lighthouse, right down to its nautical interior, with portholes and gleaming sculptures that evoke anchors and waves. Spanish chef Jorge Pereira adds Basque and Mediterranean touches to his

A Cool Scoop

There are five *paleterias* on or immediately off the zócalo, and all of them have Michoacàn in their name (this chilly, mountainous state is famous for its ice cream, and shops all over the country pay their respects, nearly without exception). These little businesses serve tourists all the time, and their product is safe, and delicious. The flavors are basically the same as you would find at home, with the exception of guava and *pasas* (prunes, with the seeds intact, be careful). Pistachio fans can look forward to huge, whole pistachios in their scoops.

4

original creations. For starters, there's a lettuce salad with goat cheese, dried wild fruits, and herb infused olive oil. Favorite main dishes are haddock with clams and seared tuna medallions with baby onions. ⊠*Elcano hotel, Av. Costera Miguel Alemán 75, Costera* ☎744/484–3100 ⚄*Reservations essential* ⊟*AE, MC, V.*

WORD OF MOUTH. "I eat in town all the time and have never had a problem . . . I don't eat weird things or uncooked foods that should be cooked. I peel my fruit, eat my yogurt and limes every day, and enjoy."–colokid

FAST FOOD

¢–$ ✕**Crepas y Churros.** A fried, sugary dessert, churros are the perfect way to top off a savory dinner before hitting one of the Costera's many bars or dance clubs. In the heart of the commercial strip, Crepas y Churros offers the usual churro options—with fillings of dulce de leche or chocolate—and for something more substantive, above-average crepes, whose silky textures strike an interesting contrast with the ever crunchy churro. ⊠*Av. Costera Miguel Alemán s/n, Costera* ☎*No phone* ⊟*No credit cards*

OLD ACAPULCO

CONTINENTAL

★ **Fodor's**Choice ✕**Coyuca 22.** This may well be Acapulco's
$$$–$$$$ most beautiful restaurant. It's like eating in a partially restored Greek ruin with a view of Doric pillars, statuary, an enormous illuminated obelisk, a small pool, and the bay beyond. Choose from two fixed menus or order à la

carte; all dishes are artfully presented. Lobster and prime rib are specialties. ⊠ *Av. Coyuca 22 10-min taxi ride from zócalo, Old Acapulco* ☎ *744/482–3468 or 744/483–5030* ⬧ *Reservations essential* ⊟ *AE, DC, MC, V* ⊘ *Closed Apr. 30–Nov. 1. No lunch.*

SEAFOOD

$$-$$$ ✕ **La Cabaña de Caleta.** In the 1950s this local favorite was a bohemian hangout that attracted renowned bullfighters along with Mexican songwriter Agustín Lara and his lady love, María Félix. You can see their photo over the bar and sample the same dishes that made the place famous back then: baby-shark tamales, seafood casserole, or shrimp prepared with sea salt, curry, or garlic. The restaurant is smack in the middle of Playa Caleta, and there are free lockers for diners who want to take a swim, as well as banana and wave-runner rentals. ⊠ *Playa Caleta Lado Ote. s/n, Fracc. las Playas, 5-min taxi ride east of town square, Old Acapulco* ☎ *744/482–5007* ⊕ *www.lacabanadecaleta. com* ⊟ *AE, MC, V*

CAFÉ

¢–$ ✕ **Los Amigos Cafè.** In an alley off the zócalo, perhaps the coolest, shadiest spot in all Acapulco, American expats Josephine and Bob Delinsky draw a crowd for their excellent $4 breakfasts. Expats are fiercely loyal to the place, and the owners are vigilant about keeping souvenir hawkers away from their clientele. In the afternoons, spare ribs, burgers, apple pie and banana splits are available, accompanied by quite excellent drip coffee. ⊠ *Calle La Paz 10, Col. Centro* ☎ *No phone* ⊟ *No credit cards* ⊘ *Closed Sun.*

MEXICAN

¢–$ ✕ **El Nopalito.** Funky and very popular, this Mexican family-run place just off the zòcalo is packed with in-the-know locals, seven days a week. The kitchen is behind a counter in the middle of the dining room, but the wide-open entries, lots of fans, and a cooling skim of water running down the back wall keep things pleasant. The chilaquiles (an entrée made with sauce over tortillas) are excellent, as are the generous $3 breakfasts and traditional Mexican lunch plates. Beer and tequila are available, and the fresh-squeezed orange juice (usually available) is most refreshing in a country that adds sugar to almost everything drinkable. The tortillas, with thin, crispy skins and soft insides, might be the best you'll find in Mexico. ⊠ *Calle La Paz 23, Centro* ☎ *744/482–1876* ⊟ *No credit cards*

ACAPULCO DIAMANTE

ECLECTIC

$$$$ ✕**Tabachin.** Elegantly ensconced within the Fairmont Pierre Marqués (where JFK and Jackie honeymooned) this red-carpeted restaurant has received a four-diamond rating from AAA since 2001, and some of the guests have been dining here nightly half the year for decades. The French-Asian fusion suits the meats and fish that are the main stand by, and the "Lifestyle Cuisine" selections feature produce exclusively from within a 50-mi radius. Eighty Mexican wines are offered, complementing the scallops, shrimp, crab, and rich desserts. A lounge combo plays late nights in the dining room, and the service is painstakingly efficient. The scallops, steamed bass, and Napoleón of beef tenderloin with pâté fois gras are all excellent. ⊠ *Av. Playa Revolcadero s/n, Col. Granjas del Marqués* ☎ *744/435–2600* ⌸ *Reservations essential* ⊟ *AE, MC, V* ⊙ *Closed Tues. in off-season. No Lunch.*

4

MEXICAN

$$$–$$$$ ✕**La Hacienda.** Giant carp drift in an ornamental pool and
★ mariachis entertain at this restaurant in a colonial hacienda, once a millionaire's estate. Chef Jorge Boneta's intriguing variations on traditional Mexican street food include rabbit enchiladas (terrific), Veracruz stuffed shrimp, and duck carnitas in a cascabel chile sauce. The pescado à la talla gives Barra Vieja a run for its money, too. On Sunday there's a champagne brunch for $30. ⊠ *Fairmont Acapulco Princess hotel, Playa Revolcadero, Revolcadero* ☎ *744/469–1000* ⊕ *www.fairmont.com* ⊟ *AE, DC, MC, V* ⊙ *Closed Mon. No lunch.*

SEAFOOD

$$$–$$$$ ✕**Pool Bar.** On a wharf that juts out into Bahía de Puerto Marqués, this casual open-air dining spot has wooden floors and a dramatic roof that simulates a huge white sail. It's particularly atmospheric after dark, when the lights of Puerto Marqués flicker in the distance. There are several fish and shellfish dishes on the menu, but the specialty is the red snapper à la talla. ⊠ *Camino Real Acapulco Diamante, Carretera Escénica, Km 14, Acapulco Diamante* ☎ *744/466–1010* ⊟ *AE, DC, MC, V.*

LAS BRISAS

ECLECTIC

★ Fodor'sChoice✕ **Baikal.** The incredible views of the Costera by
$$$$ night are just a bonus at one of Mexico's best restaurants.
Chef Pedro Linares, a native of Puebla (the home of mole)
applies his French training with a taste for streamlined
Thai cooking to create fusion dishes that do not seem
forced in the least: rather, familiar Mexican ingredients
seem to have been waiting for this treatment. The decor
is a little gaudy, but otherwise the dining experience here
nears perfection. The spinach salad appetizer with a pas-
try "bag" of figs and cheese is to die for, and the sea bass
cooked with three chilies could be the most subtle piece of
fish you've ever tasted. An extensive wine list and dessert
menu round things out. Try to resist eating too much of
the complimentary bread, which like everything else here
is flawless. There are two dinner seatings; only the first at
7 pm allows children. ✉ *Carretera Escènica 22, Las Brisas*
☎744/446–6845 ⚑*Reservations required* ▤*AE, MC, V*
⊘*Closed Mon. No lunch.*

ITALIAN

$$$ ✕**Becco al Mare.** Getting review treatment in papers as dis-
tant as the New York Times, Becco al Mare is the most
talked about new restaurant in Acapulco, both for its succu-
lent Italian food and warm modern architecture. There are
no "steals" to be had here, but the buzz is that the risotto
is the best to be had anywhere. All in all, the menu is on
the conservative side, and the standout dishes work with
seafood in from all the predictable angles. But from a lavish
dining room in the hills of Las Brisas, the meal tastes all
the more special. ✉ *Av. Carretera Escènica 14 , Las Brisas*
☎774/446–7402 ⚑*Reservations essential* ▤*MC, V*

$$$$ ✕**Casa Nova.** Live piano music lends romance to Casa
Nova, which is carved out of a cliff that rises from Bahía
de Acapulco. The views, both from the terrace and the
air-conditioned dining room, are spectacular, the service
is impeccable, and the Italian cuisine is superb. You can
choose the fixed-price *menu turístico* for $50 or order à la
carte. Favorites include lobster tail, linguine *alle vongole*
(with clams, tomato, and garlic), and *costoletta di vitello*
(veal chops with mushrooms). ✉*Carretera Escènica 5256,
Las Brisas* ☎744/446–6237 ▤*AE, MC, V* ⊘*No lunch.*

BARRA VIEJA

MEXICAN

$ ✕**Cira La Morena.** This enormous, redbrick institution is a classic seafood joint: big picnic tables, beer in bottles, and a drain in the floor for when the whole place is hosed down at the end of the day. It is said that Cira La Morena has the finest pescado à la talla in all of Acapulco. Mussels, shrimp off the barbecue or in a gigantic seafood cocktail round things out here, but it's really all about the fish. The downbeat charm will have you feeling like the first (or the last) human eating the primordial fish. ⊠ *Barra Vieja domicilio conocido, watch for sign when you get to Km 14 on Carretera Barra Vieja, Barra Vieja* ☎ *744/444–6091* ▤ *No credit cards* ✆ *Closed Mon.*

PIE DE LA CUESTA

FRENCH

$$$ ✕**Casa Blanca.** French chef Michel Fornés recently opened this beachside bistro in a stunner of a location, sharing space with the Hotel Casa Blanca. Taking a Continental approach to local fare like shrimp, mussels, and huachinango (red snapper, which is served in a roasted chile sauce and serves up to three people, for $28) and offering an excellent selection of French wines, this white-walled, Moorish-style retreat adds refinement to this (still) rural beach community. If you're just in the area for some sun, you can snack on guacamole, salsa, and tortilla chips from Casa Blanca's beach cart. ⊠ *370 Playa del Sol, Pie de la Cuesta* ☎ *744/460–0324 or 744/460–4028* ▤ *No credit cards*

MEXICAN

$$ ✕**Tres Marias.** You could sit here all day after lunch, and many do, under a big arcade facing the sea and open on all sides. Tables are pushed together for family dining over simple local specialties, and affordable ones at that. Most people come for the legendary pescado à la talla but the shrimp in garlic sauce and pollo à la brasa (grilled chicken with chiles) are excellent, too. Palapa shelters stand along the sandy side of the restaurant for those who can't bring themselves to leave the beach. ⊠ *Playa Pie de la Cuesta s/n, Pie de la Cuesta* ☎ *744/460–0178* ▤ *No credit cards* ✆ *Closed Mon.*

Beaches & Outdoor Activities

WORD OF MOUTH

"As Pixie and I were sitting by the pool [at the Mayan Palace] . . . we saw some commotion going on at the beach. A lady told us that they were releasing the baby sea turtles. I had read about this, so we rushed down to see it. Even the police were there! (For crowd control?) We caught the very end of it, where the turtles were swimming away. There was one little turtle that didn't want to swim away and I got a photo of him. So cute!"

—seattlegirl

By Grant
Cogswell

IN THE PAST FEW YEARS CITY OFFICIALS have made a great effort to clean up the Bahía de Acapulco, and maintaining it is a civic priority. Nevertheless, the best times to swim in the bay (where the beaches are safe for swimming year-round) is in the dry season from November to May. Heavy tropical rains the other half of the year make the city bloom into lushness but bring mud down from the hills as well as runoff, occasional sewage overflows, and garbage from this city of nearly a million. Although vending on the beach has been outlawed, you'll still be approached by beggars now and then, and locals hawking souvenirs, food, beer, and leisure activities of all kinds. The latter can often be a blessing: don't be put off by their unofficial demeanor, as most diving, boat trips, water and jet-skiing, parasailing, etc. are catered by very informal, one or two-person businesses. In Acapulco Bay watch for a strong shore break that can knock you off your feet in knee-deep water. It's wise to observe the waves for a few minutes before entering the water.

5

ABOUT THE BEACHES

Beaches here can be broken up into three areas: those to the west of the city; the bay itself, and those to the east. Swimming is best on the central beaches on the hotel-lined inner curve of the Costera Miguel Alemán (the street name extends past the old neighborhoods to the west, but it's this stretch that people are referring to when they say "the Costera") and on little Playas Caleta and Caletilla in Old Acapulco. For isolation, decompression, and sun, head out of the city to Pie de la Cuesta to the west, and Puerto Marqués, the hotel zone of Playa Diamante (locally known, in English, as "Princess Beach"), Playa Revolcadero, and rural Barra Vieja toward the east. For a bustling sunbath sandwiched between city and sea, enjoy the native flavor of the beaches between Parque Papagayo and the Yacht Club along the original waterfront on the west side of the bay.

The popular beaches within the city always draw a crowd—an insufferably dense one during Christmas and Easter holidays. Theft is not a great worry in the daytime with a crowd or neighbors around to keep an eye on your stuff, but the beaches should be strictly avoided at night—especially those outside the city—for safety reasons.

Hitting the Road

The Costera Miguel Alemán is the spine of the city. Named for the post–WWII Mexican president who built the six-hour highway from Mexico City and started pushing Acapulco as a world destination, the Costera is, though intimidating at first to drivers and pedestrians, actually a gentle beast (not that we recommend driving it). Motorists here, though aggressive, are extremely watchful and even rather courteous. The street itself, on which most of the tourist businesses stand, has a numbering system that makes it ridiculously difficult to find a given address (the numbers start and stop again according to the boundaries of neighborhoods, some of them very small, and with multiple or duplicate names). Asking for directions in Mexico from passersby can be a confounding time-waster: there's an ingrained hesitation to respond to a foreigner with "I don't know." Hence there is no way of knowing if the directions you might receive are based on known fact, a fairly reliable guess, or total conjecture. Taxi drivers know their way around perfectly, and will take you exactly where you want to go, but for more than you'll pay for a cab in all but the biggest resorts in Mexico. A cheaper and more colorful alternative might be the personalized, rattling International Harvester buses whose general destinations are grease-painted on their windshields. Many are kitted out with flashing disco lights, velvet curtains, and masses of stuffed animals or religious icons, and bear names like Muñeco de Oro (Golden Doll), El Jefe de Jefes (The Boss of Bosses) or the Crow. For 45¢ they provide a cheap, entertaining, and reliable trip into the real Mexico. Sit up front because the ride is bumpy in the back; for an extra 10¢ you can ride the tinted window buses with working shock absorbers, closed windows, and air-conditioning, but far less character.

WEST SIDE

★ **Fodor's Choice Pie de la Cuesta.** This surprisingly tranquil beach is close to town, wide, and very long—at the far end you might go hours without seeing a soul, even on a weekend. A casual strip of small businesses lines the road between the beach and beautiful Laguna Coyuca, a favorite spot for waterskiing, freshwater fishing, and boat rides—including to island restaurants and a nature preserve. Palapa (palm frond) shelters line the beach, offering the patrons of some excellent restaurants and hotels an idyllic space in which to relax and sunbathe—swimming is not recommended. Skilled and experienced surfers may find some waves (but no boards for rent) here, but extreme caution is advised. Buses to Pie de la Cuesta run east (counterintuitively) from the zócalo along the Costera until 10 pm, and the cost is 55¢ for the 25-minute trip.

CENTRAL

Around the point of the fort from the zócalo and the cruise ship terminal lie the most locally patronized beaches in the city. They're hugged by the busy Costera Miguel Alemán and fronted by an array of cheap fish and taco stands.

☺ **Playas Caleta and Caletilla.** On the southern peninsula in Old Acapulco, these twin, perfect little half-moon beaches face a shallow cove divided by a children's aquarium (with one of the city's best cheap restaurants). Caleta once rivaled La Quebrada as the main tourist area, and was very popular with the first jet-setters from Hollywood. The water here is perfect for snorkelers: shallow, safe, exquisitely clear in the dry months, and teeming with colorful and bizarre tropical fish. The beach mostly draws Canadian and Italian retirees, Mexican families with small children, and those wanting to take in the flavor of Old Acapulco in a relaxed and intimate, rather than urban, setting (though in a sense, you are in the very middle of town). From anywhere on the Costera, buses marked "Caleta" will get you here within minutes for 45¢. On both beaches vendors sell everything from seashell sculptures to peeled mangos. Umbrellas, chairs, and inner tubes are for rent, though unless you're going out on a boat you'll have to bring your own snorkel and mask, or buy them from the little shop under the aquarium bridge. Boats line up at the dock to ferry divers out to the strait between the Peninsula de las Playas and Isla de la Roqueta, an island nature preserve.

Playa Honda and Playa Manzanillo. These little beaches are the first of the appealingly humble parks on the east side of the bay, but they're strictly for folks coming ashore at the Yacht Club—the crowd of boats out front prevents any activity but sunbathing, and there are no facilities here. If you come by boat, though, the beaches are lovely places to picnic while enjoying the view.

Playa Dominguillo and Playa Tamarindo. Playa Dominguillo comes out from under the turnout for traffic heading to

Pie de la Cuesta and slides north under a grove of palm and tamarind trees to become Playa Tamarindo. Here the beach widens and is lined with canvas shelters, has public bathrooms, and on the little section called Karibalí, a delightful little miniature golf course.

Playa Hornos. Across from Parque Papagayo, Acapulco's largest city park, is this great front porch of the city. The plaza under the huge Mexican flag is a popular hangout for (well-behaved) local teens and workers out for a short swim, stroll, or a few hours of surfcasting.

Playa Hornitos and Playa Pretil. After the plaza at Playa Hornos, the beach swings away from the road and its character becomes far less local. Luxury hotels interact sedately with the beach, and a host of services are offered by independent guides and vendors: waterskiing ($10/hr), parasailing ($25/hr), and half-hours on wave runners ($35). Masks and snorkels are for rent, as well as umbrellas and beach chairs ($3 flat rate) outside the areas inland (behind low yellow ropes) that are the domain of the hotels. The beaches strike the perfect calm balance of diversity and singularity of purpose; family atmosphere and party; and seem to be where people are having the best time. Swimming is a little dicey, though, due to the prevalence of Jet Skis. This is also the farthest east you can enjoy soft, powdery sand.

Playa Condesa. East of Pretil lies the frisky centerpiece of the Costera. Playa Condesa is steep and the decks of tourist bars hang over the narrow strip of coarse sand. Spring Break is eternal here, with vendors, some distressingly desperate beggars, henna tattoos, bungee jumping, and two-for-one drink specials. Rocks to the east of the beach block access to **Playa Redonda**, which has one public right-of-way and is mostly the domain of the hotels on the point and the CICI aquarium.

SOUNDS LIKE ACAPULCO. Whether it's ambulatory, loudspeaker-equipped tortilla vendors at 6AM, consecutive minutes of church bell tolling early on Sunday, incessantly repetitive pitchmen hawking their wares all day from the same spot, unwanted musical accompaniment live or recorded, or all-night partying (though the noise from the zócalo stops on a dime at midnight), you can't help but notice that Mexico is a noisy country, and Acapulco might be its loudest city. There's an undeniable charm to the aura of public and commercial space here, but sometimes you'll need a break. Bring earplugs.

Playa Icacos. The last kilometer of the beach, starting at the El Presidente Hotel and before the bay ends in a navy base (which explains the empty sand farther down, and no, you can't go there) is the less crowded Playa Icacos. The breeze coming directly off the open channel into the bay is strong and will make the water choppy and pick up the fat grains of sand. This is still a good beach for kids, with a roped-off swimming area. The morning surf is especially calm.

EAST SIDE

Playa Puerto Marqués. A scenic 15-minute drive uphill—and then precipitously down—along the Carretera Escenica from Icacos will bring you to the gorgeous Playa Puerto Marqués, where aside from the jungle clinging to the bay-side cliffs, the view is very nearly Mediterranean. Bounded by a friendly neighborhood of low-rent tiendas (stores) and taquerias, this neighborhood—more than any other in Acapulco—has the relaxed, down-market atmosphere of nontourist Mexico. Boats are available for fishing expeditions and ecotours of the nearby Black Lagoon (its waters tinted by the roots of tamarind trees) of Puerto Marqués. Except for weekends, when the beach is crowded with tourists from Mexico City, the atmosphere here is the mellowest you'll find near the action of town. Ask the bus driver to let you off at the Glorieta (highway bridge), and walk or catch a cab the half-mile to the beach.

Playa Diamante. Ten minutes to the east lies a long strip set against the open sea beginning with Playa Diamante, known to locals as "Princess Beach" for the hotel that dominates it. A public access point between the hotels makes this a popular weekend spot for young Mexico City residents, who convivially root down under wide canopies to drink moderately, eat deep-fried minnows (served like French fries, with salsa or ketchup), and play Frisbee and volleyball. Swimming can be hazardous (there's a strong riptide) and isn't even very fun: a wide, foamy beach break is useless to all but the most intrepid surfers. A public restroom and showers are by the public throughway. If you drive, you'll be asked for money to watch your car, and boys will insist on carrying your things for you, also for change. Cheap colectivo vans make the run from the Glorieta, and this far out there's still a profusion of cabs

Underwater Carnival

The city has two children's aquariums: Cici Waterpark on the Playa Icacos section of the Costera, east of Condesa, and Magico Mundo, in Old Acapulco on an island between Playas Caleta and Caletilla.

Cici Waterpark (⊠*Av. Costera Miguel Alemán s/n, corner of Av. Cristóbal Colon, Costera* ☎*744/484–8210* ⊕*www.cici. com.mx* ☎*$10* ⊘*Daily 10–6*) Announcing itself in a burst of terra-cotta waves on the sidewalk of the Costera, here's one of the rare attractions in the neighborhood catering

exclusively to kids. It features a log flume ride, toddler area, wave pool, sky coaster, dolphin show, and the opportunity—for a price—to swim with the dolphins.

Magico Mundo Marina (⊠ *Playa Caleta, Old Acapulco* ☎*744/483–9344* ☎*$6* ⊘*Daily 9–6*) This small children's aquarium, much smaller-scale than Cici, has hands-on tanks full of sea life, and a sea lion show. It's also the embarkation point for glass-bottomed boats and other excursions to Boca Chica and Isla de la Roqueta.

available. This is a fun place to go for the day, but leave before the sun goes down.

Playa Revolcadero. This beach hosts a series of big hotels without a single concentrated public gathering point, and marks the beginning of the truly rural beach. It's much the same, safety-wise and in terms of rip currents, as Playa Diamante, and the miles of open beach are a great place to ride horses, which can be rented by the hour.

Barra Vieja. This is the far eastern limit of Acapulco beaches: 27 km (17 mi) from the Costera, between Laguna de Tres Palos and the Pacific. Its draws are rural isolation (increasingly encroached upon) and a splendid, sweeping sea view in a dramatic, windswept setting. If swimming is not important to you (it's too dangerous) and you're seeking solitude in the most romantic setting around, this might be your spot. A bonus is that the area is known for its delicious *pescado à la talla* (red snapper marinated in spices and grilled over hot coals).

CAUTION. Acapulco Bay is fairly well protected from the rough Pacific surf, but steep offshore drop-offs can produce waves large enough to knock you off your feet. Pay attention to the wave pattern before you go in. If you're not a strong swimmer, stay close to shore and other people. Some beaches, mostly those outside the bay such as Revolcadero and Pie de la Cuesta, have a strong surf and some have a rip current, so be careful. If you get caught in a rip current, which makes it hard to swim to shore, swim parallel to the sand. Above all, don't panic.

SPORTS & THE OUTDOORS

BASKETBALL

There's an excellent, barely used, fenced-in public basketball court on the malecón about 100 yards south (east) of the zócalo, next to the Pemex station. The court is open 24 hours a day, 365 days a year, and though unlighted, is in an area where the ambient light at night is considerable and there's plenty of foot and car traffic on the adjacent Costera for those concerned about safety.

BULLFIGHTS

The season runs from about the first week of January to Easter, and *corridas* (bullfights) are held on Sunday at 5:30. Tickets are available through your hotel or at the window in the **Plaza de Toros** (⊠*Av. Circunvalación, Playa Caleta/ Old Acapulco* ☎744/482–9561) Monday–Saturday 10–2 and Sunday 10:30–5. Tickets in the shade (*sombra*)—the only way to go—cost about $22. Preceding the fight are performances of Spanish dances and music by the Chili Frito band.

BUNGEE JUMPING

Paradise Bungy (⊠*Costera Miguel Alemán 107, Costera* ☎744/484–7529 ☜*$100 per jump* ☉*Noon until dusk*) provides an adrenaline rush and entertainment for spectators throughout the day on Playa Condesa. The 165-foot bungee-jumping tower is adjacent to the Paradise Bar.

ECOTOURISM

Although most areas both within and out of the city have an abundance of independent guides you can hire on the spot, there are a few excellent companies that provide prescheduled, all-inclusive tours leaving from hotels and the Costera, with reservations.

Coyuca Tour (⊠*Costera Miguel Alemán 116, Costera* ☎744/481–2020 ☜*$45 per person*) provides tours of Laguna Coyuca inland from Pie de la Cuesta. Kayak excursions there go to the islands in the lagoon (where a lunch of *pescado á la talla* is provided) and to the nature preserve on the lagoon's west side, where herons, pelicans, and crocodiles dwell.

A four-hour excursion to the Laguna Goyuca can also be booked with **Tourex** (⊠*Costera Miguel Alemán, Fracc. Magallanes* ☎*744/481–0508 or 744/481–0509* ⌗*$38* ⊙*Wed. and Fri. at noon, from the Costera*). Included is transport to the lagoon, lunch, and a one-hour kayak trip through the nature preserve.

Río Papagayo is 45 minutes by car from the Costera, 6 km (4 mi) south of Tierra Colorada on Highway 95, and features spectacular boulder-bound stretches of tropical river inhabited by birds and crocodiles. **Pueblo Bravo** (⊠*Av. Costera Miguel Alemán 121, Costera* ☎*744/489–1154 or 744/48–2648*) books kayak tours on the Class II plus level waters of the river.

The **Shotover Jet** (⊠*Centro Comerical Plaza Marbella, Local 17 and Av. Costera Miguel Alemán, Costera* ☎*744/484–1154* ⊕*www.shotoverjet.com.mx*) is a wild boat ride that's an import from the rivers around Queenstown, New Zealand. An air-conditioned bus takes you to the Pierre Marqués Lagoon, about 20 minutes from downtown Acapulco. Twelve-passenger boats provide thrilling 30-minute boat rides on the lagoon, complete with 360-degree turns—one of the Shotover Jet's trademarks. The cost is $45. For more thrills, from July through January, you can shoot the rapids on 1½- to 2-hour guided trips for $55; there's a four-person minimum.

Tours of the migratory bird nesting grounds at Laguna Tres Palos (just north of Playa Revolcadero and the airport) where the Río Sabana meets the Pacific are led by **Turismo Intersol** (⊠*Av. Costera Miguel Alemán 53-B, Costera* ☎*744/484–3091* ⊕*www.turismointersol.com*). They also offer a six-hour "buffet" tour of Acapulco´s historic sites, the Isla de la Roqueta, Puerto Marqués, and Tres Palmas, with a dinner of pescado á la talla and some volunteer turtle-egg collecting. The tour leaves every Monday, Wednesday, and Friday at noon on the Costera, for $60 per adult.

FISHING

Fishing is what originally drew many of the early tourists to Acapulco, and it's still an abundant area. The peak season for marlin is April–June; for tuna, April–July; mahimahi and sailfish October–March; and sharks June–October.

Carp, mullet, and catfish swim in local freshwater lagoons. The annual Acapulco International Sportsfishing Tournament takes place the last weekend of May: for information contact the Director of Tourism at ☎ *744/440–7010.*

Acapulco Scuba Center (⊠*Paseo del Pescador 13 y 14, near the zócalo, Old Acapulco* ☎*744/482–9474* ⊕*www.acapulco scuba.com*), although the name doesn't suggest it, is also an excellent place to sign up for deep-sea fishing excursions. The center's 40-foot boats accommodate up to six passengers. Trips depart at 7 AM, return at 2 PM, and cost $270 per person.

You can arrange fishing trips through your hotel or at the Pesca Deportiva on the Malecón across from the zócalo. **Fish-R-Us** (⊠*Av. Costera Miguel Alemán 100, Fracc. Las Playas, Old Acapulco* ☎*744/482–8282* ⊕*www.fish-r-us.com*) offers charter service for sailfish, tuna, and dorado fishing. Boats depart at 6 AM. You can share a boat for $70 per person, with a maximun of six people, or rent a private yacht for $370 to $440 per day.

For freshwater trips try the companies along **Laguna Coyuca**. Boats accommodating 4–10 people cost $250–$500 a day, $45–$60 by chair. Excursions leave about 7 AM and return at 1 PM or 2 PM. At the docks you can hire a boat for $40 a day (two lines). You must get a license ($12, depending on the season) from the Secretaría de Pesca; if your excursion does not include a license, there's a representative at the dock, but note that the office is closed during siesta, between 2 and 4.

GOLF

Acapulco has several world-class golf courses, mostly concentrated near Playa Revolcadero, east of the city. High afternoon temperatures make early games near-compulsory most of the year. Later in the day, breezy periods now and then make games more comfortable, if increasing the difficulty of play.

There's a short, public, well-kept golf course at the **Club de Golf** (⊠*Av. Costera Miguel Alemán s/n* ☎*744/484–0781*) on the Costera next to the convention center. Greens fees are $50 for 9 holes, $80 for 18.

Two championship courses—one designed by Ted Robinson, the other remodeled by Robert Trent Jones Sr. and then renovated under the supervision of Robert Trent Jones Jr.—are adjacent to the **Fairmont Acapulco Princess and Pierre**

Marqués hotels (⊠*Playa Revolcadero* ☎744/469–1000). Make reservations well in advance. Greens fees in high season, mid-December to mid-April, are $125 for hotel guests, $140 for nonguests. Fees are lower after noon and in low season.

A round on the 18-hole course at the **Mayan Palace** (⊠*Playa Revolcadero, domicilio conocido* ☎744/469–6000) time-share condo complex is $70 for guests, $130 for nonguests.

The excellent and newly restored 18-hole course designed by Robert Von Hagge, **Tres Vidas** (⊠*Carretera Barra Vieja, Km 7, Barra Vieja* ☎744/444–5126 or 744/444–5127 ⊕*www. tresvidas.com.mx* ⚑*$100 for 18 holes, less in off-season* ⊙*Open daylight hrs*) is dramatically set right on the beach. The distance from town thins the crowds, too.

MINI-GOLF

For miniature golf enthusiasts, **Golfito Karibalí** (⊠*Costera Miguel Alemán s/n, Playa Karibalí* ☎*No phone* ⚑*$3 per game* ⊙*10 AM until sunset, Tues.–Sun.*) is a crude but fun little course on the Karibalí section of Playa Tamarindo, across from the Gigante supermarket. A stand offers sodas and snacks as you watch the Costera rush by.

SURFING

A six-hour drive from one of the world's top surfing sweet spots (Puerto Escondido), Acapulco is not a big draw for surfers. However it's possible for beginners to enjoy the small waves on the Bahía de Acapulco, particularly at Condesa and Icacos (full-size boards are not available for rent, but boogie-boards are). Rougher open waters outside of town at Playa Revolcadero and Pie de la Cuesta draw a few intrepid souls. Entering the water in these areas, though, is for very strong and experienced surfers only. On popular stretches of beach, a flag system is in place to notify swimmers about the currents: green = safe, yellow = caution, red = don't. Playa Diamante ("Princess Beach") is right next to Revolcadero and is the area's best surfing beach, but is especially for experienced surfers only.

TENNIS

Tennis courts are exclusively concentrated in two areas: the eastern stretch of the Costera, and in the Playa Diamante/Playa Revolcadero complex east of the hill beyond Puerto Marqués. The city hosts the Mexican Open every year at the end of February at the Hotel Fairmont Aca-

Spend a Day at the Park

Parque Papagayo, ranging along the curve of the west side of the bay, and the zócalo are the twin hearts of the city. Newer, and sequestered back in the hills behind the Carretera Escenica, is the tropical canyon holding Acapulco's botanical gardens.

Jardin Botanico de Acapulco Esther Pliego de Salinas (⊠ *Av. Heroico Colegio Militar s/n, Fracc. Cumbres de Llano Largo* ☎ *744/446–5252* ⊕ *www.acapulcobotanico.org* ⌸ *$5* ⊘ *Daily dawn–dusk*) This 15-acre park occupies a canyon ranging in altitude from 600 to 1,300 feet above the bay, and features a profusion of palms, hardwoods, flowering trees and vines, as well as desert plants. Tropical parrots and iguanas inhabit the park, as well as more familiar (to Americans) eagles, raccoons, and opossum.

Parque Papagayo (⊠ *Av. Costera Miguel Alemán, between Av. Sebastián Elcano and Av. Manuel Gómez Morín, Costera* ☎ *744/485–6837* ⌸ *Free; rides $1 each; $5 ride packages available* ⊘ *Park: Daily 6* AM–*8*

PM. *Rides: nightly 4–11*) This large children's park is a relaxing place for adults and young couples, too, a kind of cross between a landscaped park and a low-rent Disneyland. It features three lakes (one has a pirate ship), paddleboats, a jogging path, two swimming pools, a petting zoo, kiddie rides, a library, carnival games, and restaurants. If you feel like you're missing the true soul and beauty of Mexico on your visit, spend some time here.

Zócalo (*Old Acapulco*) Every city and town but a handful has one in Mexico, and this is one of the very finest. The term zócalo comes from the pedestal of a long-absent flag on the Mexico City's central square; it means, literally, "pedestal." Here, fountains, a gazebo, ornamental gardens, and outdoor cafés sit under an impregnably shady canopy of banyan trees. A stroll down the steps beside the mid-20th-century cathedral into the square, as sunset awakens the bats, is one of the most evocative sights this town has to offer.

---

pulco Princess. In the high season courts are overbooked, but players will find the climate perfect for play at night, when the facilities are less crowded.

Court fees range from $9 to $26 an hour during the day and double that in the evening. At hotel courts, nonguests pay about $6 more per hour. Lessons start at about $15 an hour; ball boys get a $2 tip.

The **Grand Hotel** (⊠*Costera* ☎744/485–9050) has three hard-surface courts, two lighted. In addition to five outdoor courts, the **Fairmont Acapulco Princess** (⊠*Playa Revolcadero, Revolcadero* ☎744/469–1000) has two air-conditioned synthetic-grass, lighted indoor courts and a stadium that hosts international tournaments. The **Fairmont Pierre Marqués** (⊠*Playa Revolcadero, Revolcadero* ☎744/466–1000) has five synthetic-grass lighted courts.

Guests at the **Hyatt Regency Acapulco** (⊠*Av. Costera Miguel Alemán 1, Costera* ☎744/484–1225) have access to three hard-surface lighted courts at the Municipal Golf Club. The **Mayan Palace** (⊠*Playa Revolcadero, domicilio conocido, Revolcadero* ☎744/469–6000) condo complex has 12 lighted clay courts. There are three lighted asphalt courts at the **Park Hotel & Tennis Center** (⊠*Av. Costera Miguel Alemán 127, Costera* ☎744/485–5992). You'll find five courts at **Tiffany's Racquet Club** (⊠*Av. Villa Vera 120, Costera* ☎744/484–7949). Some are asphalt and have lights, others are clay and don't have lights. **Villa Vera** (⊠*Lomas del Mar 35, Costera* ☎744/484–0333) has two lighted clay courts and two lighted hard-surface courts.

WATER SPORTS

You can arrange to water-ski, rent broncos (one-person Jet Skis), parasail, and windsurf at outfitters on the beaches. Parasailing is an Acapulco highlight developed here in the 1960s; a five-minute trip costs $60. Waterskiing is anywhere from $10 to $40 an hour; broncos cost $40–$95 for a half hour, depending on the size. You can arrange to windsurf at Playa Caleta and most beaches along the Costera, but the best place to actually do it is at Bahía Puerto Marqués.

The clear waters (from November to May) of the Bahía de Acapulco offer excellent opportunities for diving and snorkeling, particularly in the Canal de Boca Chica between Old Acapulco's Caleta and Caletilla beaches and the island nature preserve of La Roqueta. A four-hour snorkeling excursion to Roqueta can be had from any of several pilots at the Magico Mundo dock separating Caleta and Caletilla beaches for as little as $4. The statue of the Virgen of Guadalupe fixed on the sea floor in the middle of the strait is a landmark, and bizarre attraction—the snorkeling near it is best, perhaps through divine intervention. Also of interest for divers is the 1944 wreck of the Río de la Plata off Playa Icacos: be careful, though, of Jet Ski traffic in this area.

Snorkels and masks can be rented at Icacos, and bought onshore at Caleta or rented from the boat pilots there.

Acapulco Scuba Center (✉ *Paseo del Pescador 13 y 14, near the zócalo, Old Acapulco* ☎ *744/482–9474* ⊕ *www.acapulco scuba.com*) offers four-hour snorkeling and scuba outings for beginners and certified divers. All tours include gear and round-trip transportation from your hotel. Scuba trips cost $70 with lessons and lunch included; snorkeling costs $35. The center also provides deep-sea fishing excursions.

Nightlife & the Performing Arts

WORD OF MOUTH

"A great place to grab a beer is at the zócalo, where you can sit and watch the people go by from any of the tables set up on the plaza, or from the second floor of the restaurant La Flor de Acapulco."

—krbr17

By Grant
Cogswell

ACAPULCO'S NIGHTLIFE IS LEGENDARY FOR SEVERAL REASONS. In a poor country, it has been a playground of the Mexican elite for more than 60 years, enthralling the imaginations of the less privileged. There are still echoes of the city's time as a druggy, decadent stopover for rock glitterati and Euro jet-set aristocracy in the 1970s. And just as consistent as the wealthy at play is the overwhelming general friendliness of the Mexican people and their adeptness at letting their hair down and having a really good time. The dream-imagery of a chain of luxury hotels glittering like a jeweled necklace at night, reflected in one the loveliest bays on Earth, is just icing on the cake.

As soon as the sun sets, Acapulco's party life emerges from the hotels or comes back from the beach to eat and window-shop on the Costera until 11 PM, when the clubs begin to fill. The party really does go on until dawn, or 4 AM on an early night. Playa Condesa is the loud epicenter of public festivity, with its bungee jumping, loud bands, and open-air beachside bars. Acapulco's glamour is in the club zone on the Carretera Escénica, above the city to the east. Admission to this demimonde can be costly, but it's something to try at least once. The resorts occasionally offer entertainment with big-name artists, or at least live music during happy hour, as well as restaurant theme parties or dancing at a beach bar. On the zócalo, you'll find torch singers and mariachis belting out Mexican soul music.

ABOUT THE NIGHTLIFE & THE PERFORMING ARTS

The casual open-air bars are mostly without cover, and shorts and T-shirts are common attire. Drinks cost $2–$5, and most places have two-for-one drink specials at happy hour. The waiters depend on tips in the 15%–20% range: the high end of this is expected in the more expensive clubs, which charge from $15 up to $100 for entry, sometimes including drinks and sometimes not. Women usually pay less than men. Dress up to go out anywhere but the beach and the bars of La Condesa—for all of this country's casual atmosphere, Mexicans are extremely formal dressers. You'll want to take a cab to clubs on the Carretera Escénica, along most of which there are no sidewalks or streetlights. Mexico's legal drinking age is 18.

Though long a vacation spot or winter home for wealthy Mexicans and North Americans and possessing the atmosphere of a (small) "world city," Acapulco lacks a substantial infrastructure for the fine arts. Galleries are strictly commercial, and classical and folk concerts, plays, and dance perfor-mances take place in just two multipurpose locations.

BARS

COSTERA

★ **Baby Lobster Bar** (⊠*Av. Costera Miguel Alemán near Bungee Jump in La Condesa* ☎*744/484–1096* 🔊*No cover*), an open-air spot on the beach is frequented primarily by tourists. There's a two-for-one special on beer and well-drinks when you arrive and the rowdy atmosphere is extremely conducive to meeting others. Tabletop dancing is not discouraged, especially late at night. There's no cover, so patrons can come and go from the other bars immediately adjacent on the Condesa strip.

You're supposed to—and can—feel like you're on the deck of a pirate ship here at **Barbarroja** (⊠*Av. Costera Miguel Alemán 107 A, La Condesa* ☎*744/484–5932* 🔊*No cover* 🕒*Daily noon–3* AM). The theme is a little worn (perhaps the bar is pursuing El Galeon down the bay), but on a strip of neon and garish pastels, this multilevel bar, open to the stars and built of dark wood, is something of a relief, standing out despite no flashing lights and visual clutter. The deck is much longer than it is wide, so when cover bands come to play, at midship with their backs to the sea and the speakers pointing across the 30 feet to the sidewalk, it gets loud.

As the name suggests, **Disco Beach** (⊠*Playa Condesa, Costera* ☎*744/484–8230* 🔊*Cover is $30, including drinks*) is right on the sands. It's so informal that most people turn up in shorts. The waiters are young and friendly—some people find them overly so, and in fact, this is a legendary pickup spot. Every Wednesday is ladies' night, when all the women receive flowers. "Foam parties"—for which the entire dance floor fills up with suds—reign on Friday.

Not to be confused with the other Lobster Bar, **La Langosta Felíz** ("The Happy Lobster") ⊠*Av. Costera Miguel Alemán 2121, La Condesa* ☎*744/484–1922* 🔊*No cover* 🕒*6* PM–*4*AM, *closed Mon.*) is the one with the giant plastic cartoon lobster out front. The dance floor is practically right on the surf; the music is a fun and funky mix of reggaetón (Mexican reggae/rap), popular hip-hop and party-rock, hosted with a sense of wacky fun: free drinks for hat-wearers at 1 AM and the nightly "Cascada de Espuma" at 2 AM, when suds fill the dance floor, and the revelry ascends as clothes are peeled

6

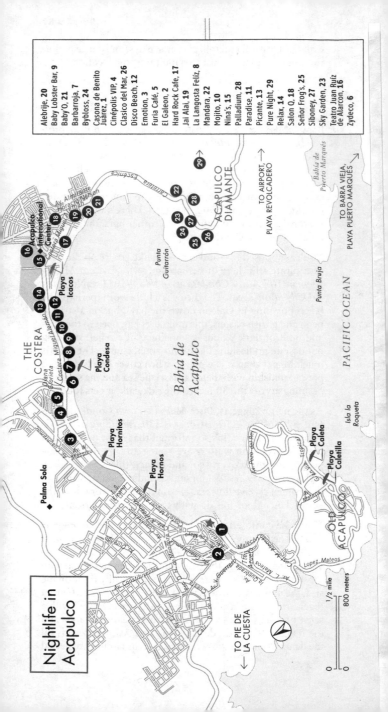

Nightlife in Acapulco

Alebrije, 20
Baby Lobster Bar, 9
Baby0, 21
Barbarroja, 7
Bybloss, 24
Casona de Benito Juárez, 1
Cinépolis VIP, 4
Clasico del Mar, 26
Disco Beach, 12
Emotion, 3
Furia Café, 5
El Galeon, 2
Hard Rock Cafe, 17
Jai Alai, 19
La Langosta Feliz, 8
Mandara, 22
Mojito, 10
Nina's, 15
Palladium, 28
Paradise, 11
Picante, 13
Pure Night, 29
Relax, 14
Salon Q, 18
Señor Frog's, 25
Siboney, 27
Sky Garden, 23
Teatro Juan Ruiz de Alarcon, 16
Zydeco, 6

off to reveal swimsuits and the dancing becomes much more escandaloso (it's a foam party, what do you expect?).

★ The restaurant occupying the bottom floor of **Paradise** (⊠*Av. Costera Miguel Alemán 101, Costera, near Fiesta Americana Hotel* ☎*744/484–5988* ⚏*No cover*) is an open, triple-decker beamed building—like a SoHo warehouse with the brick and drywall skinned off—and has beach access, a swimming pool, and lively dance contests at night. The open-air bar upstairs affords a spectacular bay view and it's the perfect vantage point for the clientele (young, sunburned, and drunk) to watch bungee jumpers as they plunge from the platform next door.

OLD ACAPULCO

If you're looking for a pleasant place for drinks near the zócalo, your choices are few and far between. The high-ceilinged **El Galeon** (⊠*José María Iglesias 8, Centro* ☎*744/480–0001* ⚏*No cover* ⊘*5 PM-3 AM, closed Mon.*) is decorated in an Armada theme, but isn't cheesy—other than the brass cannons looming over the sidewalk, it's a normal bar with a jukebox of rock and Mexican banda music, clean and friendly with decent tacos, spaghetti, and breaded fish. Women won't be uncomfortable here.

CARRETERA ESCÉNICA

If you're out with a crowd of diverse ages and tastes, **Señor Frog's** (⊠*Carretera Escénica 28, Fracc. Playa Guitarron* ☎*744/446–5734 or 744/446–5735* ⊕*www.senorfrogs.com* ⚏*No cover* ⊘*Daily 10 AM–1 AM*) is a good fallback—it might be a cookie-cutter bar, but it can at least accommodate you. Crowded cliffside with Bybloss and Sky Garden, **Señor Frog's** has branches in every resort in Mexico, makes quality Mexican food and burgers, and is also known for its "upside-down margarita" specialty, in which the waiter will get the drinker into a headlock and shake them like a maraca, making the world feel even more topsy-turvy in their booze-addled mind. This franchise serves pozole (pork stew) every Thursday as dictated by national tradition, and radio hits from the '70s and '80s play on the sound system.

BETTING

COSTERA

Small, well-lighted, and low-key, **Emotion** (⊠*Av. Costera Miguel Alemán 224, Fracc. Magallanes* ☎*744/486–7022* ⚏*No cover* ⊘*Daily 10 AM—3 AM*), a gambling hall close to the shopping paradise of Galerias Diana, feels more like a bar that has sprouted an inordinate number of slot and video poker machines. Bingo is played all day long.

Jai Alai (⊠ *Av. Costera Miguel Alemán, Icacos* ☎744/484– 3163 ⊴$3 ⊙*Daily 10* AM–*3* AM) a Basque version of lacrosse and popular with Mexican gamblers, is played nearly nonstop in this concrete cube next to Wal-Mart. Bettors watch from behind glass as they wager. Bingo and slots are also available.

DANCE CLUBS

PARTY WITH THE DEVIL. During the fever pitch at Acapulco's clubs around 3 am on Sunday, a bizarre and startling event can take place that is not to be missed: the Devil appears. For the past several years, he's been calling on the clubs Mandara and Palladium and in the form of a very tall and athletic young man with classical Indian features, covered in silver body paint and dressed in an Aztec warrior costume (he's also known as "the Aztec") with a giant feather headpiece. As he lip-synchs along to the late Detroit ghettotech impresario Disco D's club hit "Dance with the Devil," the crowd cheers him on and goes wild. Bare description does not do justice to the mad infectiousness of this performance—if you can keep your booty still or stop a grin from covering your face, you're indeed no match for "the Devil."

COSTERA

A huge club hiding behind a deceptively narrow exterior, **Alebrije** (⊠ *Av. Costera Miguel Alemán 3308, across from Hyatt Regency, Costera* ☎744/484–5902 ⊴*Cover: $25 women, $35 men, including drinks*) can accommodate 5,000 people and attracts a younger (late teens, early twenties) crowd. From 10:30 to 11:30 PM, the music is slow and romantic (there are plenty of booths and settees to recline and canoodle upon); afterward you'll hear dance music from contemporary pop to tropical and move beneath light shows until dawn.

Small, expensive, and exclusive, **Baby'O** (⊠ *Av. Costera Miguel Alemán 22, Costera* ☎744/484–7474 ⊴*Cover: $30 women, $60–$100 men, not including drinks*) has a long history of catering to the local elite. Amid the steel and glass of the Costera, its fake-rock, Land of the Lost exterior is hard to miss and the jungle-inspired interior is over-the-top.

It's hard to get in (some wait for hours outside), and even harder to get a table, but this is *the* place in Acapulco to go to see and be seen, so dress sharp. It's closed Sunday and Monday in low season (May through November).

Zydeco (✉ *Av. Costera Miguel Alemàn 121, Local 15, Fracc. Magallanes, Costera* 🕾 *744/484–5775 or 744/484–5774* 🕾 *No cover* ⊘ *1* PM *– 2* AM *Closed Mon.*), a club rare for its intimate vibe on the mid-Costera, is eclectically decorated with enamel walls, shuttered windows, and chandeliers to give it a plantation feel. A young crowd is drawn to its unassuming vibe and disco, pop, electronica, house, and trance music

CARRETERA ESCÉNICA

This elegant pillbox hat perches on the side of the Carretera Escénica, the classy opposite of its neighbor Señor Frog's. **Bybloss** (✉ *Carretera Escènica 28, Centro Comercial La Vista, Fracc. Playa Guitarròn* 🕾 *744/446–5727 or 744/446–5728* ⊕ *www.bybloss.com.mx* 🖅 *$20–$40, drinks not included* ⊘ *9* PM *-4* AM. *Closed Mon.*) is a full-service dinner-and-nightclub and has columns supporting high beams and long, modernist chandeliers: the swanky surroundings don't stop the bar from serving tacos, though. DJs spin an eclectic mix of house beats, electronica, and a smattering of boisterous Mexican pop mixing hip-hop and banda.

It may take some time to get through the door of the exclusive **Mandara** (✉ *Carretera Escènica s/n, Fracc. Guitarròn* 🕾 *744/446–5711 or 744/446–5712* ⊕ *www.acapulcomandara.com* 🖅 *$30–$40, drinks not included* ⊘ *10:30* PM *–6* AM. *Closed Mon.*) in the hills above the Costera, and if you aren't dressed to the nines, you won't. Although this is meant to engender the vibe of a VIP lounge, because this is Mexico, people are just as friendly as they are anywhere else. If you want to club-hop, the looser Palladium is virtually next door. House, electronica, and trance rule the night.

★ **Fodor's**Choice A waterfall cascades down between the five terraced dance floors of **Palladium** (✉ *Carretera Escènica, Fracc. Guitarròn* 🕾 *744/446–5490* 🖅 *Cover: $16–$26 women, $26–$36 men, including drinks*) considered by many to be Acapulco's best for ambience (2,000-person capacity, 50-foot-high windows with a wraparound view of the city), music (20,000 watts of power), and extras (a free drink on Saturday, fireworks shooting off the roof at 4 AM, and a performance by "The Devil" on Saturday ⇨ *Party with the Devil, above*). The club is so popular that you may face a wait to get in.

This roof-party of a lounge bar emerges from an open-walled penthouse with couches scattered on a comfortable, palm-studded terrace. **Sky Garden** (⌗*Carretera Escènica 128, Local 1, Fracc. Playa Guitarròn* ☎*744/446–5690 or 744/446–5892* ⊕*www.skygarden.com.mx* ⌗*$20–$30 cover, drinks not included* ☉*7 PM–4 AM. Closed Mon.*) is like the chillout room of a rave (purple lights and the night sky and view of Costera). The dance party featuring mostly house and electronica begins very late.

ACAPULCO DIAMANTE

One of the more exclusive clubs by virtue of location (an upscale windowless cube clear out nearly to the airport, past Acapulco Diamante), **Pure Night** (⌗*Calle Manzana 43, Boulevard de los Naciones* ☎*744/466–3101* ⌗*$30–$50, drinks not included* ☉*10 PM–6 AM. Closed Mon.*) is a good choice for those who want to settle down in a hideaway and dance rather than club-hop. The music includes disco and pop hits.

LAS BRISAS

Facing the sea from high in the exclusive, hilly neighborhood of Las Brisas resort from which this area takes its name, **Clasico del Mar** (⌗*Carretera Escènica Lote ·2-A, Las Brisas* ☎*744/44–6475* ⌗*Cover $20–$40, drinks not included* ☉*9 PM–4 AM. Closed Mon.*) and its disco and popular oldies from the '70s, '80s, and '90s pull a decidedly older crowd than most of the Carretera's booty-shaking palaces. When not dancing, you can relax on comfortable circles of sofas, viewing the lights of the Costera.

GAY BARS

COSTERA

Come late to this double-decker disco right behind Carlos n' Charlie's on the Costera. **Picante** (⌗*Privada de Piedra Picuda 16, Fracc. Club Deportivo* ☎*744/484–2342* ⌗*$7* ☉*Thurs.–Sun. 10 PM–6 AM*) is large, loud, and spicy: male strippers appear Saturday but the venue is for both gays and lesbians.

The more punk-rock, down-and-dirty underground of Acapulco's major gay venues, **Relax** (⌗*Lomas del Mar 4, Fracc. Club Deportivoalongside Office Max on the Costera* ☎*No phone* ⌗*$10 cover* ☉*Wed.–Sun. 9 PM–4 AM*) doesn't even have a phone, but it does feature a nightly drag show and fills up even later than Picante. The floors and stairs are painted entirely black, so watch your step.

LIVE MUSIC

LATINO

COSTERA

Furia Café (⊠*Paseo del Farralon 5, Fracc. El Farralon* ☎*744/484–2179* ✆*$3–$16* ☉*Daily 1* PM*–4* AM) .

A diverse crowd dances nightly in this glass-walled, classy spot stuck in among the cheesier no-cover bars of La Condesa. At **Mojito** (⊠*Av. Costera Miguel Alemán s/n, La Condesa* ☎*744/484–8274* ✆*$10 cover* ☉*8* PM*–2* AM) icy mojitos and sweet rum drinks honor the Cuban heritage of salsa, the house musical genre, and keep things festive as patrons dance feverishly to a nightly schedule of smoking-hot bands. It's usually closed on Monday.

A cavernous red box of a venue, plunked down a little mysteriously among shop windows and raucous bars on the sidewalk of the Costera, **Nina's** (⊠*Av. Costera Miguel Alemán 2909, Fracc. Costa Azul* ☎*744/446–5490* ✆*$22, drinks included* ☉*7* PM*–3* AM) hosts huge live salsa shows with celebrity impersonators (a normal combination in these parts) and attracts the best and most enthusiastic dancers in town of all ages.

The so-called Cathedral of Salsa, **Salon Q** (⊠*Av. Costera Miguel Alemán 3117, Costera* ☎*744/481–0114* ✆*Cover: $24*) is a combination dance hall and disco, where the bands play salsas, merengues, and other Latin rhythms for young and old. Weekends include shows featuring impersonations of Mexican entertainers.

Hard Rock Cafe (⊠*Av. Costera Miguel Alemán 37, Fracc. Costa Azul* ☎*744/484–0047 or 744/484–6680* ⊕*www.hardrockcafe.com* ✆*Cover for some shows* ☉*Daily noon–2* AM) is surprisingly the only venue in town for smalltime, mainstream Mexican rock bands. (Acapulco is not on either the alternative or the stadium rock and hip-hop tour circuit.) When appearing here, virtually all bands play covers of the most popular (in Mexico) American and English classic rock tunes as well as the biggest native rock hit-makers like Maná and Café Tacúba. Like any other Hard Rock, memorabilia makes the decor.

6

CARRETERA ESCÉNICA

What the stunningly romantic nighttime view of the Costera lights from the Carretera Escénica really calls for is this: languid piano interpretations of jazz and popular standards. At **Siboney** (⊠*Carretera Escénica 28 Local 1, Fracc. Guitarrón* ☎*744/446–5711* ⊕*www.acapulcosiboney.com* ⛁*$10–$20, drinks not included* ☉*Tues.–Sun. 6 PM–3 AM*) lounge revivalists will find a smooth cognac goes well with the atmosphere.

MOVIES

COSTERA

With 15 screens, **Cinèpolis VIP** (⊠*Galerias Diana, Av. Costera Miguel Alemán, Fracc. Magallanes, Costera* ☎*744/484–9070* ⊕*www.cinepolis.com.mx* ⛁*$5 adults* ☉*Daily 11 AM–midnight*) at the top of an American-style mall on the Costera is one of the few places to boast a decent selection of feature films in English (with subtitles in Spanish, rather than dubbing) in all of Mexico. The air-conditioning is blessedly fierce.

PERFORMANCE VENUES

Casona de Benito Juárez (⊠*Calle Benito Juárez s/n, at Calle Felipe Valle, Centro* ☎*744/483–5104* ⊕*www.acapulco.gob. mx* ⛁*Varies* ☉*Open for events only*) makes Acapulco's tiny arts scene seem all the more precious. On the schedule you might find touring flamenco performers, Mexican folklorico companies (performing traditional songs and dances), or chamber music ensembles.

The city's main (and fully modern) theater inside the convention center on the far west side of the Costera, **Teatro Juan Ruiz de Alarcon** (⊠*Av. Costera Miguel Alemán 4455, Costera* ☎*744/455–0130* ⊕*www.centroacapulco.com* ⛁*Varies* ☉*Open for events only*) has a capacity of 1,100 people. Local repertory and touring musicals and plays are on the schedule, as well as regular concerts by soloists and the Acapulco Philharmonic Orchestra.

Acapulco Philharmonic Orchestra (☎*744/484–6626* ⊕*www.filarmonicadeacapulco.org.mx* ⛁*Free*) plays a free concert every two or three weeks at the Teatro Juan Ruiz de Alarcon from February through July (see Web site for concert schedule). Founded in 1998, the orchestra features guest players from all over Latin America and is known for their rendition of Carl Orff's Carmina Burana.

Shopping

WORD OF MOUTH

"And for those of you traveling US domestic—just simply do not purchase anything liquid prior to going through security. It simply does not matter that the packaging is sealed from a store.

If you really want to purchase that Coffee Liquor, Hot Sauce, Perfume, Mango Jam, etc.—then plan to pack it in your checked bags and hope it doesn't break.

—dfarmer

By
Jonathan
J. Levin

GUERRERO STATE IS KNOWN FOR HAND-PAINTED CERAM-ICS, objects made from *palo de rosa* wood, bark paintings depicting scenes of village life and local flora and fauna, and embroidered textiles. Stands in downtown's sprawling municipal market are piled high with handicrafts, as well as fruit, flowers, spices, herbs, cheeses, seafood, poultry, and other meats. Practice your bargaining skills here or at one of the street-side handicrafts sellers, as prices are usually flexible. The best way to get a good price is to pit vendors against one another in a bidding war for your business. Talk to as many of them as possible, and let them see that you're a savvy customer, not a gullible tourist.

Boutiques selling high-fashion Mexican designs for men and women are plentiful and draw an international clientele. This is a great place to shop for bathing suits, evening wear, and gems from all over the world. Many shops also sell high-quality crafts from throughout the country, like wood animals and black pottery from Oaxaca, blown glass from Jalisco, and a wide range of ceremonial masks. Although many of Acapulco's stores carry jewelry and other articles made of silver, aficionados tend to make the three-hour drive to the colonial town of Taxco—one of the world's silver capitals.

The vendors that stroll up and down Acapulco's beaches generally are selling subpar merchandise for over-the-top prices. Be warned that once you buy something from one of them, others will come and linger at your side until you buy something else.

ABOUT THE SHOPPING
Most shops are open Monday–Saturday 10–7, though it's not uncommon for shopkeepers to close at 5 pm and reopen their doors around 7 PM to the crowds beginning their bar crawls. The main strip is along Avenida Costera Miguel Alemán from the Costa Club to El Presidente Hotel. Here you can find Guess, Peer, Aca Joe, Amarras, Polo Ralph Lauren, and other sportswear shops, as well as emporiums like Aurrerá, Gigante, Price Club, Sam's, Wal-Mart, Comercial Mexicana, and the upscale Liverpool department store, Fabricas de Francia. Old Acapulco has jewelry from Taxco, as well as inexpensive tailors and lots of souvenir shops. In general, the farther you get from the Costera, the less likely you are to be treated like a tourist—in other words, the less likely you are to face price gouging. The Golden Zone (Zona Dorada) encompasses the Costera and the inland area behind it called Centro.

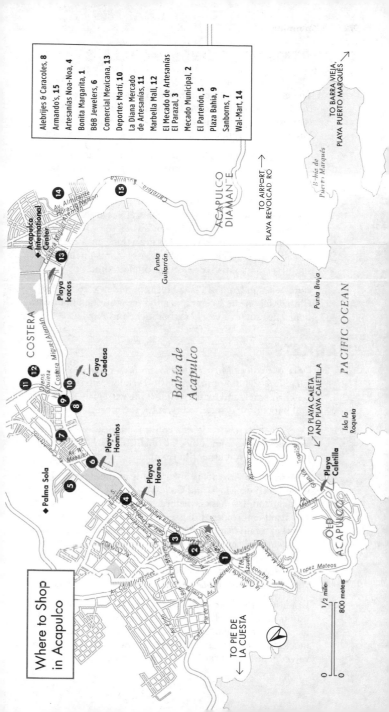

Where to Shop in Acapulco

Alebrijes & Caracoles, **8**
Armando's, **15**
Artesanías Noa-Noa, **4**
Bonita Margarita, **1**
B&B Jewelers, **6**
Comercial Mexicana, **13**
Deportes Marti, **10**
La Diana Mercado
   de Artesanías, **11**
Marbella Mall, **12**
El Mecado de Artesanías
   El Parazal, **3**
Mecado Municipal, **2**
El Partenón, **5**
Plaza Bahia, **9**
Sanborns, **7**
Wal-Mart, **14**

ACAPULCO
DIAMANTE

TO AIRPORT →
PLAYA REVOLCADRO →

TO BARRA VIEJA,
PLAYA PUERTO MARQUÉS →

Bahía de
Puerto Marqués

PACIFIC OCEAN

Punta
Guitarrón

Punta Bruja

Bahía de
Acapulco

Playa Icacos

COSTERA

Playa Condesa

Playa Hornitos

Playa Hornos

Palma Sola

Acapulco
International
Center

Av. Almirante
Horacio Nelson

Ciudad Miguel Alemán

Costera Miguel Alemán

Av. W. Massieu

Diana Glorieta

Acapulco International Center

Playa
Caletilla

Playa
Caleta

TO PLAYA CALETA
AND PLAYA CALETILLA ←

Isla la
Roqueta

OLD
ACAPULCO

Av. Pozo del Rey

Av. Gran Vía Tropical

Av. Mateos

López Mateos

TO PIE DE
LA CUESTA ←

0   1/2 mile
0   800 meters

DEPARTMENT STORES, MALLS & ARCADES

The major scenes of commerce are along the Costera, or the Golden Zone. **Aca Mall**, next door to Marbella Mall, is all white and marble and filled with the likes of Tommy Hilfiger, Peer, and Aca Joe.

The multilevel **Marbella Mall**, at the Diana *glorieta* (traffic circle) on the Costera, is home to Martí, a sporting-goods store; a health center (drugstore, clinic, and lab); the Canadian Embassy; Bing's Ice Cream; and several restaurants.

The Mexican department store chain **El Nuevo Mundo** (⊠*102 Avenida Cuauhtemoc, Golden Zone* ☎*744/486–6131* ⊕*www.elnuevomundo.com*) has everything a traveler could possibly need in clothing, shoes, toys, and linen, with a slightly less exhaustive selection of electronics.

Plaza Bahía, in front of Playa Hornitos and next to the Costa Club hotel on the Costera, is an air-conditioned mall with boutiques such as Dockers, Nautica, and Aspasia.

MARKETS

Dalia (⊠*Costera Miguel Alemán, Golden Zone* ☎*No phone* ⊙*Daily 9–9*) has approximately 60 vendors offering sweets, beach apparel, and crafts. Vendors are extremely aggressive and bargaining is required even for the most minor items.

One large flea market with a convenient location is **La Diana Mercado de Artesanías**, a block from the Emporio hotel, close to the Diana monument in Costera.

El Mercado de Artesanías El Parazal is at the intersection of Calle Cinco de Mayo and Calle Vásquez de León. Look for fake ceremonial masks, the ever-present onyx chessboards, $20 hand-embroidered dresses, imitation silver, hammocks, and skin cream made from turtles (don't buy it, because turtle harvesting is illegal in both Mexico and the United States, and you won't get it through U.S. Customs). From Sanborns downtown, head away from Avenida Costera to Vásquez de León and turn right one block later. The market is open daily 9–9.

Don't miss the **Mercado Municipal**, where restaurateurs load up on produce early in the morning, and later in the day locals shop for piñatas, serapes, leather goods, baskets, hammocks, amulets to attract lovers or ward off enemies, and velvet paintings of the Virgin of Guadalupe.

CLOSE UP

Mementos of Acapulco

So you're going down to Mexico and you want to bring back something that will serve as a reminder of your trip. Well we've been out there, braving the crowds, and have found some choice picks for you.

Silver. While the silver town Taxco can't be beat for selection, the shops in the zócalo area of Acapulco offer you much of the same merchandise for competitive prices. If you don't mind crowds of tourists, Bonita is an excellent little shop in which to pick up a necklace or a set of earrings.

Masks. Much as Oaxaca is known for its black pottery and Jalisco is known for its blown glass, the state of Guerrero is renown for its mask-making tradition, which dates back some 3,000 years. Masks representing everything from Aztec folk images to political unrest can be found in Acapulco's markets, with Mercado de Parazal boasting one of the better selections.

Cocadas and tamarindos. Vendors throughout the city sell candies called cocadas and tamarindos, made from coconut and tamarind respectively. Much like fudge and taffy at East Coast shores, these sweet indulgences wrapped in festive "Acapulco" packaging can serve as a pleasant reminder of your trip even months after the fact. Typically, the tamarindos come in two varieties: the spicy red tamarindos, which are eaten, and the sweet brown tamarindos, which are dissolved in water to make a juice drink.

A bungee photograph. You might not cliff dive but you can jump from Acapulco's famed bungee platform. The platform is right in the center of the main drag, and you'll feel like a celebrity as you plunge toward the pool below. Moreover, the pictures you'll take home—for an extra $20—will be proof of perhaps your bravest feat.

NEED A BREAK?

Close to the bungee platform on the Costera, Tacos Orientales is a great place to grab tacos after a night at the dance club. Except for its marginally offensive logo—a caricature of an Asian man—this restaurant has nothing to do with anything "oriental." But the tacos are good by anyone's standards, and the service is remarkably efficient, even at the wee hours of the night (or morning).

7

Across from the Plaza Bahia mall, the vendors in the **El Pueblito** (⊠*Pizzaro and Costera Miguel Alemán, Golden Zone* ☎*No phone* ☯9 AM–7 PM) outdoor market sell a lot of mass-produced souvenirs like T-shirts and sombreros.

The market's best fixtures are its antojito restaurants, where you sample delicious local cuisine at great prices.

GROCERIES

If you plan on cooking in your suite or villa, the king-size supermarket chain **Comercial Mexicana** (⊠ *Costera Miguel Alemán y Pascual Cervera s/n, Golden Zone* ☎744/484–2927 ⊕*www.comercialmexicana.com* ⊙*Daily 8 AM–11 PM*) has everything you'll need, including familiar brands at reasonable prices. There are also plenty of free samples.

Members of **Sam's Club** (⊠*516 Avenida Farallón, b/w Golden Zone and Las Brisas* ☎744/469–0202 ⊕*www. sams.com.mx* ⊙*Weekdays 10–8:30, Sat. 9:30–8:30, Sun. 10–6*) enjoy the same prices on groceries and appliances in Acapulco as they do at home. Of course, everything comes in bulk, so you won't want to shop here unless you plan on staying in Mexico for a while.

SPECIALTY SHOPS

ART GALLERIES

This Costera gallery of **Edith Matison's** (⊠ *Costera Miguel Alemán 2010, Acapulco Diamante* ☎744/484–3084 ⊙*Mon.–Sat. 10 AM–2 PM, 5 PM–9 PM*) emphasizes the work of Mexico's better established artists, many of them famous the world over.

Stop in the **Esteban Art Gallery** (⊠*Scenic Hwy., Balcones #110-2, next to Madieras restaurantCostera* ☎744/446–5719 ⊕*www.esteban-acapulco.com*) to see the works of renowned international and Mexican artists, including Calder, Dalí, Siqueiros, and Tamayo. Some crafts are also sold.

Galería Rudic (⊠*Calle Vicente Yañez Pinzón 9, Costera ✛Across from Continental Plaza and adjoining Jardín des Artistes restaurant* ☎744/484–1004) represents top contemporary Mexican artists, including Armando Amaya, Gastón Cabrera, Trinidad Osorio, and Casiano García.

The Hungarian artist, **Pal Kepenyes**, (⊠*Guitarrón 140, Lomas Guitarrón* ☎744/484–3738) who lives in Mexico, gets good press for his jewelry and sculpture (some of it rather racy), on display in his workshop.

Guadalajara-based **Sergio Bustamante** (⊠*Av. Costera Miguel Alemán 120–9, across from Fiesta American Condesa hotel,*

Costera ☎744/484–4992 ✉*Hyatt Regency Acapulco, Av. Costera Miguel Alemán 1, Costera* ☎744/469–1234) is known for his whimsical, painted papier-mâché and giant ceramic sculptures.

BOOKS & MUSIC

This Mexican chain store **Cristal** (*Cuauhtémoc 27, Golden Zone* ☎744/483–5191 ⊕*www.libreriasdecristal.com. mx* ☺*Weekdays 10* AM–8 PM) offers leisure and academic books, all of them conveniently searchable on the company's computer network. Books are predominantly in Spanish, although a small number of English and other foreign language texts are on hand.

In La Gran Plaza Mall in the Golden Zone, **La Feria del Disco** (✉*Costera Miguel Alemán 1632, Golden Zone* ☎744/486–6479 ☺*Daily 10* AM– 9 PM) has a wide selection of music to choose from, including all the Latin pop hits you heard at those Costera dance clubs.

The chain **El Partenón** (✉*Av. Cuahutemoc 412, Golden Zone* ☎744/482–4084 ⊕*www.elpartenon.com.mx*), near Papagayo Park, offers books, office supplies, and computers. There's a limited selection of English and other foreign language books.

CLOTHING

Armando's (✉*Hyatt Regency Acapulco, Av. Costera Miguel Alemán 1, Costera* ☎744/484–5111 ✉*Av. Costera Miguel Alemán 1252–7, in La Torre de Acapulco, Costera* ☎744/469–1234) sells its own line of women's dresses, jackets, and vests with a Mexican flavor. It also has some interesting Luisa Conti accessories.

As you know, great shoes are the centerpiece of a great outfit. **El Campeón** (✉ *Juan R Escudero No. 13 A1, Old Acapulco* ☎744/483–8412 ☺*10* AM–7PM) sells bold kicks made out of materials like alligator skin.

The trendy line of beachwear sold at **Cusma** (✉ *Costera Miguel Alemán, s/n, Golden Zone* ☎ *No phone* ☺ *10* AM–7 PM) can help equip the entire family for a day in the sun.

International celebrities and important local families are among the clientele of ritzy **Esteban's** (✉ *Scenic Hwy., Balcones #110-2, next to Madiera's restaurant, Costera* ☎744/446–5719 ⊕*www.esteban-acapulco.com*). Its opulent evening dresses range from $200 to $3,000; daytime dresses average $120. There's a men's clothing section on the second floor. If you scour the sale racks you can find some items marked down as much as 80%.

Factory Outlet Havaina and Cobian (⊠ *Urdaneta #1, Golden Zone, Fraccionamiento Hornos* ☎744/486–3078 ⊘*Mon.– Sat. 10 AM–6 PM*) only sells sandals, offering the popular brands Arraia, Dupe, Yarena, and Cobian at great prices.

Tommy Hilfiger (⊠*17 Costera Miguel Aleman, Golden Zone* ☎744/484–3325 ⊕*www.tommy.com.mx*) features a full line of mostly casual men's wear, with an emphasis on warm weather apparel.

HANDICRAFTS

A good place for gifts, **Alebrijes & Caracoles** (⊠*Plaza Bahía, Costera* ☎744/485–0490) consists of two shops designed to look like flea-market stalls. Top-quality merchandise includes papier-mâché fruits and vegetables, Christmas ornaments, wind chimes, and brightly painted wooden animals from Oaxaca.

Arte Para Siempre (⊠*Av. Costera Miguel Alemán 4834, near Hyatt Regency Acapulco, Costera* ☎744/484–2390), in the Acapulco Cultural Center, sparkles with handicrafts from the seven regions of Guerrero. Look for hand-loomed shawls, painted gourds, hammocks, baskets, Olinalá boxes, and silver jewelry.

As in many handicraft places in Acapulco, most of what you'll find at **Artesanías Noa-Noa** (⊠*Costera Miguel Alemán, Old Acapulco* ☎744/486–2078) are mass-produced trinkets, not art. Nevertheless, they make for fun reminders of your trip to the glitzy town.

Mi Casita (⊠*Plaza Bombay, local 7, Fraccionamiento Costa Azul, Acapulco, 39580, Costa Azul* ☎*No phone* ⊘*Mon.– Sat. 10 AM–8 PM*). Aptly named—Mi Casita translates to "My Little House"—this shop specializes in handcrafted miniatures of churches and houses, all of them charming reminders of a trip to Acapulco.

TOYS & PARTY SUPPLIES

In business for some 20 years, **El Abuelo** (⊠*Calle, Mina, 389, San Jose* ☎744/84–2423 ⊘*9 AM–6:30 PM*) is a large novelty store and costume shop that has everything you need to throw an impromptu party in Acapulco, or a Mexican-theme fiesta at home.

Happy Toys (⊠ *Centro Comercial Galerías Diana Locala, 21 Costera Miguel Alemán esq. Pinzón, Golden Zone*

☎744/481–3982 ⊕*www.happytoys.com.mx* ☺*Mon.–Sat.
9 AM–7 PM*) is a major retailer that offers toys and games
for children of all ages.

PHOTOGRAPHY

In the basement of the Gigante (a countrywide supermarket
chain selling both imported and domestic products), **Foto
Imagen** (✉ *Cristobal Colón No, Golden Zone* ☎744/484–
3770 ☺*Mon.–Sat. 10 am–7 pm*) offers a full range of services for your digital and film prints,

If you have any problems with your digital or analogue
camera, **TCF Tecnifoto** (✉ *Centro Comercial Constituyentes,
Av. Constituyentes 247, Old Acapulco* ☎744/483–8316
☺*Mon.–Sat. 9 AM–7 PM*) is a good place to go for a quick and
thorough repair. They'll also develop your film, burn your
digital prints to a CD, or even restore old photographs.

SILVER & JEWELRY

You can watch craftsmen at work at **B and B Jewelers** (✉*Parque
Papagayo on Av. Costera Miguel Alemán* ☎744/485–6270),
a huge store and jewelry factory in Papagayo Park. Authentic gold jewelry and fire opals are specialties.

SILVER SECRETS. Buy silver and jewelry made from semiprecious
stones only in reputable establishments, or you might end up
with cleverly painted paste or a silver facsimile called alpaca.
Make sure that 0.925 is stamped on the silver piece; this veri-
fies its purity.

A favorite stop of Acapulco tour groups, **Bonita Margarita**
(✉*Ignacio de la Llave 2, Old Acapulco* ☎744/482–0590
☺*10 AM–7 PM*) serves potential customers free margaritas
while they peruse the selection of jewelry, leather, and
crafts, much of it from the state of Guerrero. As is usually
the case in Acapulco, you'll only get a good price if you're
prepared to bargain.

To encourage business, **Joyería Plaza Taxco** (✉*Quebrada
74, Golden Zone* ☎744/482–3428) provides free transportation to and from its Centro location—call and they'll
arrange a van to pick you up. They offer a wide selection
of rings, bracelets, and necklaces in conservative designs,
and they promise to have alterations and custom designs
completed within 48 hours.

Diamond jewelry of impeccable design by Charles Garnier
and Nouvelle Bague is sold at **Minette** (✉ *Fairmont Aca-*

pulco Princess hotel arcade, Playa Revolcadero, Revol-cadero ☎744/469–1000). There's also jewelry set with Caledonia stones from Africa as well as Emilia Castillo's exquisite line of brightly colored porcelainware inlaid with silver fish, stars, and birds

Orfebres Linda de Taxco (✉ *Av. Costera Miguel Aleman 1926, Golden Zone* ☎744/483–3347 ⊕*www.lindadetaxco.com. mx* ☉*Mon.–Sat. 10 am–6 pm*). With bold contemporary designs, this Taxco-based chain now has a location right in the heart of Acapulco in the Galerias Diana.

The exquisite flatware, jewelry, and objets d'art that can be found at **Tane** (✉*Las Brisas hotel, Carretera Escénica 5255, Las Brisas* ☎744/469–6900) were created by one of Mexico's most prestigious (and pricey) silversmiths.

SPORTING GOODS

Featuring all the name brands, the sporting goods superstore **Deportes Martí** (✉*Fracc. Faraión del Obispo Glorieta de la Diana, Golden Zone* ☎744/484–5733 ⊕*www.marti.com. mx* ☉*Mon.–Sat. 10* AM*–7* PM) is the best place to load up on camping and rafting gear before venturing out into the local wilderness. As with electronics and other brand name goods, expect to pay as much as double what you would pay in the United States.

SUNDRIES

A countrywide institution, **Sanborns** is a good place to find English-language newspapers, magazines, and books; basic cosmetics and toiletries; and high-quality souvenirs. All branches are open 7 AM–1:30 AM in high season and 7:30 AM–11 PM the rest of the year. ✉*Av. Costera Miguel Alemán 1226, Golden Zone*☎744/484–4413 ✉*Av. Costera Miguel Alemán 3111, Golden Zone*☎744/484–2025 ✉*Av. Costera Miguel Alemán 209, Golden Zone*☎744/482–6167 ✉*Av. Costera Miguel Alemán off Zócalo, Old Acapulco* ☎744/482–6168.

Wal-Mart (✉*500 Costera Miguel Alemán, Fracc. Club Deportivo* ☎744/469–0203 ⊕*www.walmartmexico.com. mx* ☉*Daily 10–10*) on the Costera has a convenient parking garage, a hair salon, and a laundromat on the premises.

Souvenirs aside,**Woolworth's** (✉*Avenida Cuauhtémoc, no. 629, Traditional Zone l* ☎744/482–0082 ☉*10* AM*–9* PM) offers good prices for clothes, beauty products, and any other essentials you might have forgotten to pack.

Side Trip to Taxco

WORD OF MOUTH

"Took a taxi to the *teleférico* (cable car) on the edge on town, giving great photo ops of the town and surrounding mountains and valley. Taxco is a wonderful small town, very picturesque, and a great place to visit. Of course the wife bought some silver jewelry!"

—Pugosan

Updated
by
Claudia
Rosenbaum

IN MEXICO'S PREMIER "SILVER CITY," 275 km (170 mi) north of Acapulco, marvelously preserved white-stucco, red-tile-roof colonial buildings hug cobblestone streets that wind up and down the foothills of the Sierra Madre. Taxco (pronounced *tahss*-ko) is a living work of art. For centuries its silver mines drew foreign mining companies. In 1928 the government made it a national monument. And today its charm, abundant sunshine, flowers, and silversmiths make it a popular getaway.

The town's name was derived from the Nahuatl word *tlacho* meaning "the place where ball is played." Spanish explorers first discovered a wealth of minerals in the area in 1524, just three years after Hernán Cortés entered the Aztec city of Tenochtitlán, present-day Mexico City. Soon Sovácon del Rey, the first mine in the New World, was established on the present-day town square. The first mines were soon depleted of riches, however, and the town went into stagnation for the next 150 years. In 1708 two Frenchmen, Francisco and Don José de la Borda, resumed the mining. Francisco soon died, but José discovered the silver vein that made him the area's wealthiest man. The main square in the town center is named Plaza Borda in his honor.

After the Borda era, however, Taxco's importance again faded, until the 1930s and the arrival of William G. Spratling, a writer-architect from New Orleans. Enchanted by the city and convinced of its potential as a center for silver jewelry, Spratling set up an apprentice shop. His talent and fascination with pre-Columbian design combined to produce silver jewelry and other artifacts that soon earned Taxco its worldwide reputation as the Silver City once more. Spratling's inspiration lives on in his students and their descendants, many of whom are today's famous silversmiths.

Taxco's biggest cultural event is the Jornadas Alarconianos, which honors one of Mexico's greatest dramatists with plays, dance performances, and concerts in the third week of May. Other fiestas provide chances to honor almost every saint in heaven with music, dancing, and fireworks. A refreshing change is the Día del Jumil each November on the first Monday after the Day of the Dead, when the townsfolk climb the Cerro del Huixteco to capture jumil beetles and fry them up for snacks, or grind them into salsa. Taxco is on the side of a mountain, 5,800 feet above sea level, and many of its narrow, winding streets run nearly vertical. So bring some good walking shoes and be prepared to get some lung-gasping exercise.

GETTING HERE & AROUND

To visit Taxco at your own pace, perhaps including an overnight stay, arrange to rent a car in Acapulco and enjoy the scenic drive to the mountain town. The trip takes 3½ hours via the toll road and about 45 minutes longer on the more scenic free road. If you can start early, consider taking the scenic road to get there and the toll road to return. Both roads are sparsely populated between the two cities. Warning: On the toll road there are very few opportunities to turn around. Once in Taxco, follow the signs to the *centro* (center). You can usually find street parking near the zócalo. You may be approached by people who can help you find parking for about 10 pesos. Estrella buses leave Acapulco for Taxco five times a day from 7 AM to 6:40 PM from the Terminal Central de Autobuses de Primera Clase (First-Class Bus Terminal). The cost for the approximately 4½-hour ride is about $15 one-way. Grupo Estrella Blanca buses depart from Acapulco several times a day from the Terminal de Autobuses. Purchase your tickets at least one day in advance at the terminal if it's a Mexican holiday or Christmas week. A first-class, one-way ticket is $15. Buses depart from Taxco four times a day.

ESSENTIALS

Bus Contacts First-class **Estrella de Oro** (✉ *Av. Cuauhtémoc 1490, Acapulco* ☎ *744/485–8758* ✉ *Av. de los Plateros 386, Taxco* ☎ *762/485–8705 or 762/622–0648*). **Grupo Estrella Blanca** (✉ *Av. Ejido 47, Old Acapulco, Acapulco* ☎ *744/469–2017* ✉ *Av. de los Plateros 310, Taxco* ☎ *762/622–0131*).

8

EXPLORING

❶ Iglesia de San Sebastián y Santa Prisca has dominated the busy,
★ colorful Plaza Borda since the 18th century. Usually just called Santa Prisca, it was built by French silver magnate José de la Borda in thanks to the Almighty for Borda's having literally stumbled upon a rich silver vein, although the expense nearly bankrupted him. According to legend, St. Prisca appeared to workers during a storm and prevented a wall of the church from tumbling. Soon after, the church was named in her honor. The style of the church—a sort of Spanish baroque known as churrigueresque—and its pale pink exterior have made it Taxco's most important

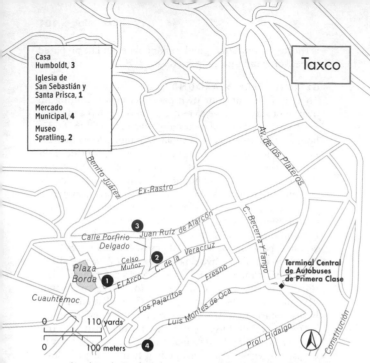

Casa
Humboldt, **3**

Iglesia de
San Sebastián y
Santa Prisca, **1**

Mercado
Municipal, **4**

Museo
Spratling, **2**

Taxco

landmark. Its facade, naves, and *bovedas* (vaulted ceilings), as well as important paintings by Mexican Juan Cabrera, are slowly being restored. ⊠*Southwest side of Plaza Borda* 🕾*No phone* ⊙*Daily 6 AM–9 PM.*

NEED A BREAK? Around Plaza Borda are several *neverías (ice-cream stands)* where you can treat yourself to ice cream in such exotic flavors as tequila, corn, avocado, or coconut. **Acerto,** fondly known as Bar Paco, directly across the street from Santa Prisca, is a Taxco institution; its terrace is the perfect vantage point for watching the comings and goings on the zócalo while sipping a margarita or cold beer.

② The former home of William G. Spratling houses the **Museo Spratling,** which displays some 140 of the artist's original designs plus his collection of pre-Columbian artifacts. Exhibits also explain the working of colonial mines. ⊠*At the Plazuela de Juan Ruíz de Alarcón plaza on Calle Porfirio Delgado 1* 🕾*762/622–1660* 🎫*$2.70* ⊙*Tues.–Sun. 9–3.*

③ **Casa Humboldt** or Museo de Arte Virreinal, as it is also known, was named for German naturalist Alexander von

Humboldt, who stayed here in 1803. The Moorish-style 18th-century house has a finely detailed facade. It now contains a wonderful little museum of colonial art. ⊠*Calle Juan Ruíz de Alarcón 12* ☎762/622–5501 ⊠*$1.50* ☉*Tues.–Sat. 10–6, Sun. 10–4.*

★ **Fodor's**Choice Saturday and Sunday mornings locals from surrounding towns come to sell and buy produce, crafts, and everything from peanuts to electrical appliances at the **Mercado Municipal.** It's directly down the hill from Santa Prisca. Look for the market's chapel to the Virgin of Guadalupe.

OFF THE BEATEN PATH **GRUTAS DE CACAHUAMILPA.** Mexico's largest caverns, the Caves of Cacahuamilpa are about 30 km (19 mi) northeast of Taxco. English-speaking guides will lead you along a 2-km (1 mi) illuminated walkway in large chambers with fascinating geological formations. A tour takes around two hours. ⊠*$4.50 (includes tour)* ☎721/104–0155 ☉*Daily 9–5.*

WHERE TO EAT

You can find everything from tagliatelle to iguana in Taxco restaurants, and meals are much less expensive than in Acapulco. Dress is casual.

¢–$$$ ✕ **Señor Costilla.** The Taxco outpost of the zany Carlos Anderson chain, known for joke menus and entertaining waiters, serves barbecued ribs and chops. Get here early for a table on the balcony overlooking the main square. ⊠*Plaza Borda 1* ☎762/622–3215 ▭*MC, V.*

¢–$$ ✕ **Hostería el Adobe.** This intimate place has excellent food ★ and hanging lamps and masks. There are meat and fish dishes, but the favorites are garlic-and-egg soup and the *queso adobe,* fried cheese on a bed of potato skins, covered with a green tomatillo sauce. ⊠*Plazuela de San Juan 13* ☎762/622–1416 ▭*MC, V.*

¢–$$ ✕ **El Mural.** You can eat indoors or out on a poolside terrace ★ where there's a view not only of a Juan O'Gorman mural but of the stunning Santa Prisca church. The chef prepares international beef and seafood dishes as well as Mexican specialties like cilantro soup and crepes with *huitlacoche* (corn fungus, a pre-Hispanic delicacy that is counterintuitively delicious). The daily three-course, fixed-price meal is $25. For breakfast try the home-baked sweet rolls and marmalade from the fruit of nearby trees. ⊠*Posada de la*

8

CLOSE UP

One Man's Metal

In 1929 the writer-architect William Spratling arrived from New Orleans and settled in the then sleepy, dusty village of Taxco because it was inexpensive and close to the pre-Hispanic Mexcala culture that he was studying in Guerrero Valley.

For hundreds of years Taxco's silver was made into bars and exported overseas. No one even considered developing a local jewelry industry. Journeying to a nearby town, Spratling hired a couple of goldsmiths and commissioned them to create jewelry, flatware, trays, and goblets from his own designs. Ever the artist with a keen mind for aesthetics, Spratling decided to experiment with silver using his designs. Shortly afterward, he set up his own workshop and began producing highly innovative pieces. By the 1940s Spratling's designs were gracing the necks of celebrities and being sold in high-end stores abroad.

Spratling also started a program to train local silversmiths; they were soon joined by foreigners interested in learning the craft. It wasn't long before there were thousands of silversmiths in the town, and Spratling was its wealthiest resident. He moved freely in Mexico's lively art scene, befriending muralists Diego Rivera (Rivera's wife, Frida Kahlo,

wore Spratling necklaces) and David Alfaro Siqueiros as well as architect Miguel Covarrubios. The U.S. ambassador to Mexico, Dwight Morrow, father of Anne Morrow who married Charles Lindbergh, hired Spratling to help with the architectural details of his house in Cuernavaca. American movie stars were guests at Spratling's home; he even designed furniture for Marilyn Monroe.

When his business failed in 1946, relief came from the United States Department of the Interior: Spratling was asked to create a program of native crafts for Alaska. This work influenced his later designs. Although he never regained the wealth he once had, he operated the workshop at his ranch and trained apprentices until he died in a car accident in 1969. A friend, Italian engineer Alberto Ulrich, took over the business and replicated Spratling's designs using his original molds. Ulrich died in 2002, and his children now operate the business.

Spratling bequeathed his huge collection of pre-Hispanic art and artifacts to the people of Taxco, and they're now displayed in a museum carrying his name. The grateful citizens also named a street after their much-beloved benefactor and put a bust of him in a small plaza off the main square.

Misión, Cerro de la Misión 32 ☎762/622–0063 ☰AE,
MC, V.

★ **Fodor'sChoice** ✕**La Parroquia.** The balcony at this pleasant
¢–$$ café offers an outstanding view of the plaza and cathedral.
Enjoy a too-much-tequila cure—the $4 Mexican breakfast
of *huevos parroquia*—and watch the town come to life. Or
come in for a beer as the sun sets over the zócalo. ✉*Plaza
Borda* ☎762/622-3096 ☰MC, V.

¢–$ ✕**Santa Fe.** Mexican family-type cooking at its best is served
in this simple restaurant a few blocks from the main square.
Puebla-style mole, Cornish hen in garlic butter, and enchila-
das in green or red chili sauce are among the tasty offerings.
There's a daily *comida corrida* (fixed-price) meal for $6.50.
✉*Calle Hidalgo 2* ☎762/622-1170 ☰*No credit cards.*

WHERE TO STAY

Taxco has two main types of hotels: small inns nestled in
the hills around the zócalo and larger, more modern hotels
on the outskirts of town.

$$$–$$$$ ▦ **Posada de la Misión.** Laid out like a colonial style village,
★ this hotel has well-kept doubles with beamed ceilings and
two-bedroom suites; some come with fireplaces and ter-
races as well. The pool area has a mural by noted Mexican
artist Juan O'Gorman, and there's a silver workshop and
boutique that sells Spratling-designed silver jewelry. **Pros:**
Beautiful view, interesting architecture. **Cons:** Too pricey
for what you get, not well up-kept. ✉*Cerro de la Misión 32*
✉A.P. 88, 40230 ☎762/622-0063 ⊕*www.posadamision.
com* ⌂*120 rooms, 30 suites* ⌂*In-room: no a/c, kitchen
(some). In-hotel: restaurant, bar, pool, no elevator, parking
(no fee)* ☰AE, MC, V ⓘMAP.

$$–$$$ ▦ **Hotel de la Borda.** It may be a bit worn, but the Borda
is still a favorite with tour groups, and the staff couldn't
be more hospitable. Ask for a room overlooking town or
the suite that John and Jackie Kennedy occupied during
their honeymoon in Mexico. **Pros:** View overlooking the
Santa Prisca Cathedral. **Cons:** Needs refurbishing. ✉*Cerro
del Pedregal 2* ✉A.P. 6, 40200 ☎762/622-0025 ⊕*www.
taxcohotel.com* ⌂*110 rooms, 3 suites* ⌂*In-hotel: restau-
rant, room service, bar, pool, no elevator, laundry service,
parking (no fee)* ☰AE, MC, V ⓘEP.

8

$$–$$$ 🏨 **Monte Taxco.** A colonial style predominates at this full-service hotel, which has a knockout view, a funicular, three restaurants, a disco, and nightly entertainment; it's the fanciest hotel in Taxco. There are also rooms equipped for guests with disabilities. **Pros:** Funicular is an amazing way to arrive at your digs. **Cons:** A few miles up a mountain from town, so plan to take taxis to get back and forth. ✉*Lomas de Taxco* ✆*A.P. 84 40210* ☎*762/622–1300* ⊕*www.monte taxco.com.mx* ⤳*153 rooms, 6 suites, 32 villas* ⌂*In-hotel: 3 restaurants, golf course, tennis courts, pools, gym, laundry service, parking (no fee)* ⊟*AE, MC, V* ⚟*EP.*

$–$$ 🏨 **Hotel Victoria.** With its colonial-style architecture, the Victoria is a perfect fit for this charming town. Its simple rooms are attractive and freshly painted. Most have balconies with great views of town and the distant hills. Furniture in the common areas was designed by William Spratling. **Pros:** Dreamy architecture. **Cons:** Parts are in disrepair. ✉*Calle Carlos J. Nibbi 5* ✆*A.P. 83, 40200* ☎*762/622–0004* ⊕*www.victoriataxco.com* ⤳*63 rooms, 5 suites* ⌂*In-hotel: restaurant, bar, pool, no elevator, parking (no fee)* ⊟*AE, MC, V* ⚟*EP.*

¢–$$ 🏨 **Posada San Javier.** The secluded San Javier sprawls haphazardly around a jungle-like garden with a pool and a wishing well. In addition to guest rooms, there are seven one-bedroom apartments with living rooms and kitchenettes; however, these are often filled by visiting wholesale silver buyers. **Pros:** Breakfast included, professionally run. **Cons:** No elevator. ✉*Calle Estacadas 32 40200* ☎*762/622–3177* ✍posadasanjavier@hotmail.com ⤳*18 rooms, 7 apartments* ⌂*In-room: kitchen (some). In-hotel: restaurant, room service, bar, pool, no elevator, parking (no fee)* ⊟*MC,V* ⚟*EP.*

¢   🏨 **Hotel Los Arcos.** This 1620 converted monastery is an island of historical tranquility. Simple, ample-size rooms furnished with colonial hand-carved furniture provide a comfortable stay just a block from the plaza. The hotel doesn't have a restaurant or gift shop, but given its central location they aren't needed. **Pros:** Lovely courtyard, intriguing history. **Cons:** No breakfast, rooms on the street can be noisy. ✉*Juan Ruíz de Alarcón 440200* ☎*762/622–1836* ⊕*www.hotellosarcos.net* ⤳*21 rooms* ⌂*In room: no a/c, no phone. In-hotel: no elevator* ⊟*No credit cards.*

¢   🏨 **Hotel Emilia Castillo.** Rooms at this straightforward hotel are simple but with carved-wood furniture and Mexican artwork that was clearly chosen with care. The brick and stone lobby has warm red-tile floors, cheerful murals, and its very own silver shop. With a restaurant just outside the front door, and attentive and friendly service, this restaurant is as practical as it is an excellent value. **Pros:** Appealing décor, intimate feeling. **Cons:** Smallish rooms, overall very compact. ⊠*Juan Ruíz de Alarcón 7* ☎762/622–1396 ⊕*www.hotelemiliacastillo.com* ⤳*14 rooms* ⏸*In-room: no phone. In hotel: no elevator* ⊟*DC, MC, V* ⓸*EP.*

NIGHTLIFE

The **Acerto** (⊠*Plaza Borda 12* ☎762/622–0064), also called Bar Paco, is a traditional favorite and a great place to meet fellow travelers. At **Bertha's** (⊠*Plaza Borda 9* ☎762/622–0172), Taxco's oldest bar, a tequila, lime, and club soda concoction called a Bertha is the specialty. Watch out for Taxco's high curbs and ankle-turning cobblestones after a few Berthas. **La Pachanga** (⊠*Cerro de la Misión 32* ☎762/622–5519), a discotheque at Posada de la Misión, is open Thursday through Sunday and is popular with townsfolk and visitors. Much of Taxco's weekend nighttime activity is at the Monte Taxco hotel's discotheque, **Windows** (⊠*Lomas de Taxco* ☎762/622–1300). On Saturday night the hotel has a buffet and a fireworks display.

SHOPPING

Sidewalk vendors sell lacquered gourds and boxes from the town of Olinalá as well as masks, straw baskets, bark paintings, and many other handcrafted items. Sunday is market day, which means that artisans from surrounding villages descend on the town, as do visitors from Mexico City.

Most people come to Taxco with silver in mind. Three types are available: sterling, which is always stamped 0.925 (925 parts in 1,000) and is the most expensive; plated silver; and the inexpensive *alpaca,* which is also known as German or nickel silver. Sterling pieces are usually priced by weight according to world silver prices. Fine workmanship will add to the cost. Bangles start at $4, and bracelets and necklaces cost $10 to $200 and higher.

Many of the more than 600 silver shops carry identical merchandise; a few are noted for their creativity. William Spratling, Andrés Mejía, and Emilia Castillo, daughter of renowned silversmith Antonio Castillo, are among the famous names. Designs range from traditional bulky necklaces (often inlaid with turquoise and other semiprecious stones) to streamlined bangles and chunky earrings.

CRAFTS

Joyería y Máscaras Arnoldo (⊠*Calle Palma 1* ☎762/622–1272) has ceremonial masks; originals come with a certificate of authenticity as well as a written description of origin and use. For $100 per person, Arnoldo will take you on a tour of the villages where the dances using the masks are performed on February 2 and December 12. **D'Elsa** (⊠*Plazuela de San Juan 13* ☎762/622–1683), owned by Elsa Ruíz de Figueroa, carries a selection of native-inspired clothing for women and a well-chosen selection of crafts.

SILVER

★ FodorsChoice **Emilia Castillo** (⊠*Juan Ruíz de Alarcón 7, in the Hotel Emilia Castilla* ☎762/622–3471) is one of the most exciting silver shops; it's renowned for innovative designs and for combining silver with porcelain. (Neiman Marcus sells the wares in its U.S. stores.) The stunning pieces at **Galería de Arte en Plata Andrés** (⊠*Av. de los Plateros 113A, near Posada de la Misión* ☎762/622–3778 ⊕*www.andres artinsilver.com.mx*) are created by the talented Andrés Mejía. He showcases his own designs and those of such promising young designers as Priscilla Canales, Susana Sanborn, Francisco Diaz, and Daniel Espinosa, whose jewelry has been loved by many a Hollywood celebrity.

★ **Spratling Ranch** (⊠*South of town on Carretera Taxco–Iguala, Km 177* ☎762/622–6108) is where the heirs of William Spratling turn out designs using his original molds. You can shop only by appointment.

Ixtapa & Zihuatanejo

WORD OF MOUTH

"[Zihua] is where almost all the Mexicans live that work in Ixtapa . . . Playa Municipal [is] the beginning of a nice walk along the curved buy area. From here you can walk along a board walk to Playa La Madera and on to Playa La Ropa . . . as you walk, keep the water to your right hand side. Playa La Ropa is the jewel of the area with its mile long curve of soft sand bordering the bay."

—Percy

Updated
by Carissa
Bluestone

ALTHOUGH THEY COULDN'T BE MORE DIFFERENT, Ixtapa (eesh-*tah*-pa) and Zihuatanejo (zee-wha-ta-*NEH*-ho) are marketed together as a single resort destination, and both have gorgeous bays and beaches. Zihua, as it's often called, was a remote fishing village with minimal tourist traffic for hundreds of years. Ixtapa was created in the 1970s when Mexico's National Fund for Tourism Development (FONOTUR) cleared away a coconut plantation. Though both are still very laid-back, they have attracted so much attention (and building) that "purists" are now heading 25 minutes north to the surfing enclave of Troncones or 35 minutes south to the more low-key fishing village of Barra de Potosi.

Although Ixtapa is quite pleasant, and self-sufficient in terms of services, its designers were unable to give it a heart and soul. A pretty marina with a few upscale sea-food restaurants at the northern end of town is the only "attraction"; other than that Ixtapa is simply a long line of beachfront resorts. Many visitors head 7 km (4 mi) south to enjoy the more authentic ambience of Zihua. There are plenty of beachfront hotels, and the cluster of pedestrian-only streets close to the marina is very touristy. That said, tourism hasn't completely destroyed Zihua's small-town essence—it's the friendliest of the Pacific Coast's major resort areas.

GETTING HERE & AROUND

Aeropuerto de Zihuatanejo is 12 km (8 mi) southeast of Zihua. Private cab fares range from $22 to $29. The bus station is in Zihua, with service to Manzanillo (8–9 hours), Acapulco (7 hours), Morelia (3½ hours), and Mexico City (7 hours).

Driving south from Manzanillo on Carretera 200 is a gorgeous seven-hour trip that twists along mostly undeveloped coast. The four-hour Zihua–Acapulco leg on Carretera 200 passes through small towns and coconut groves.

Minibuses run every 10–15 minutes between the Ixtapa hotels and downtown Zihua until 10 PM; the fare is about 50¢. Cabs (unmetered) are easy to hail on the street in Zihua; the fare to Ixtapa is $4–$5. In town, a car only comes in handy if you plan to take day trips, as cab fares can be expensive (as much as $25 one way to Troncones from Ixtapa's resorts).

ESSENTIALS

Bus Contacts Estrella Blanca (⊠*Office in Centro Comercial Los Patios, Ixtapa* ☎755/554–3474).**Estrella de Oro** (⊠*Ticket office in Plaza Ixpamar, Ixtapa* ☎755/554–2175)

Medical Assistance Hospital General de Zihuatanejo (⊠*Av. Morelos s/n, at Mar Egeo, Zihuatanejo* ☎755/554–3965). **Police** (☎755/554–2040). **Red Cross** (☎755/554–2009). **Tourist Police** (☎755/554–2207).

Visitor & Tour Info Guerrero State Tourism Office (⊠*Paseo de los Golondrinas 1-A, Blvd. Ixtapa s/n, Ixtapa* ☎755/553–1967). **Oficina de Convenciones y Visitantes** (*[Convention and Visitors' Bureau]* ⊠*Paseo de las Gaviotas 12, Ixtapa* ☎755/553–1570 ⊕*www.visit-ixtapa-zihuatanejo.org*).

EXPLORING

IXTAPA

The primary hotel zone, la Zona Hotelera, extends along a 3-km (2-mi) strip of sandy beach called Playa del Palmar. It's fun to walk along the shore to check out the various hotel scenes and water-sports activities. Swimming is so-so because of how the small waves break close to shore. You can walk the length of the same zone on the landward side of the hotels, along Paseo Ixtapa. This landscaped thoroughfare—essentially, Ixtapa's only main street—is an access road that feeds the hotels on one side and strip malls filled with restaurants on the other. It's nicely landscaped and includes a broad path for pedestrians and cyclists. The Zona Hotelera's southerly end is also home to the 18-hole Palma Real Golf Club; at the resort's northwest end is the anemic Marina Ixtapa development.

BEACHES

★ Fodor'sChoice **Isla Ixtapa.** The most popular spot on Isla Ixtapa (and the one closest to the boat dock) is Playa Cuachalalate. An excellent swimming beach, it was named for a local tree whose bark has been used as a remedy for kidney ailments since ancient times. A short walk across the island, Playa Varadero hugs a rocky cove. Guides recommend snorkeling here, but watch for coral-covered rocks on both sides of the cove. Just behind is Playa Coral, whose calmer, crystal-clear water is more conducive to swimming. Each of the above beaches is lined with seafood eateries eager to rent snorkel equipment. Playa Carey, toward the island's south end, is

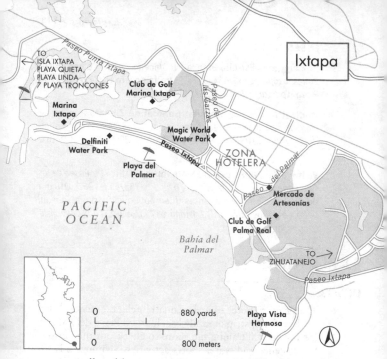

small and has no services. Pangas (skiffs; $4 round-trip) run between the boat landings at both Cuachalalate and Varadero beaches and Playa Linda on the mainland, where you'll find a few all-inclusive, high-rise hotels.

Playa del Palmar. Ixtapa's main beach, this broad, 3-km-long (2-mi-long) stretch of soft brown sand runs along the Zona Hotelera. Although you can swim here, small waves break right onshore and currents are sometimes strong. Each hotel offers shaded seating on the sand. Concessions rent Jet Skis ($40 per half hour), Hobie Cats ($50 per day) and arrange banana-boat rides (15 minutes costs $5 per passenger with a four-person minimum) and parasail trips ($25 for a little more than 10 minutes). Licensed guides in white uniforms cruise up and down selling horseback-riding and boating tours. Women offer hair braiding and massage under open-sided tents.

Playa Linda. Thatch-roof restaurants dispense beer, soda, and the catch of the day just north of the Qualton Inn, in the Zona Hotelera II. Mexican families favor this long, coconut-palm-lined beach, which has beautiful views, is perfect for walking, and is bordered at one end by an estuary with birds and gators. You can rent horses (about half as much here as on Playa Ixtapa or from area tour operators), and a warren of identical stalls sells souvenirs and cheap plastic beach toys. Concessions arrange banana-boat rides and rent Jet Skis and Boogie boards. Water taxis depart here for Isla Ixtapa, and land taxis wait in the free parking lot for fares.

Playa Quieta. Club Med occupies the south end of tranquil Playa Quieta; the rest of the lovely cove is empty except for a cluster of tables and chairs that picnicking families rent for the day for a small fee, and the equally unobtrusive Restaurant Neptuno, which sells reasonably priced seafood all week.

GIDDYUP! Most area tour operators arrange guided horseback excursions on Playa Linda and Playa del Palmar. Costs are high ($35–$40 for roughly 1½ hours), but they include transportation and usually a soft drink or beer after the ride.

ZIHUATANEJO

Everything in Zihuatanejo radiates out from the main beach. Although this stretch of sand is not the place for swimming, it's the best place to get a sense of the timeless local rhythm. Fishermen still set off in outboard-motorized skiffs and return a few hours later to sell their catch right there on the beach. A few blocks down, companies on and around the municipal pier, or *muelle*, take tourists on half- or full-day fishing adventures of their own, or on a 10-minute trip across the bay to one of the best swimming and snorkeling beaches, Playa las Gatas. The pier also marks the beginning of the Paseo del Pescador (Fishermen's Walk), or malecón. Follow this seaside path, only a third of a mile long, along the main beach which is fronted by small restaurants and shops. Along the way you'll pass the basketball court that doubles as the town square.

The malecón ends at the **Museo Arqueológico de la Costa Grande** (⊠*Paseo del Pescador 7 at Plaza Olof Palme* ☎755/554–7552), a gray stone building identified with a wooden shingle. A permanent display of pre-Hispanic murals, maps, and archaeological pieces trace the history of the so-called Costa Grande (Grand Coast) through the colonial era. It's open Monday–Saturday 10–6; admission is $1. Beyond the museum, a footpath cut into the rocks leads to Playa la Madera.

Zihuatanejo

DOWNTOWN

Mercado de Artesanía

Museo Arqueológico de la Costa Grande

Paseo del Pescador

Mercado Municipal

Benito Juárez
5 de Mayo
Avenida
N. Alvarez
AV.

Playa Principal

Municipal Pier

TO IXTAPA
TO AIRPORT

Playa la Madera

Camino Escénico a Playa la Ropa

Playa la Ropa

Bahía de Zihuatanejo

Playa las Gatas

TO PLAYA LARGA

0   1,000 yards
0   1,000 meters

WORD OF MOUTH. "Ixtapa is a beautiful beach resort—not as big as Cancún—and Zihuatanejo is a very charming fishing village just a few miles from Ixtapa. The night life is great, and the weather is perfect." –ponchotj

BEACHES

★ **Playa las Gatas.** Legend has it that a Tarascan king (from an indigenous, pre-Hispanic community) built the breakwater on Playa las Gatas to create a sheltered area for his daughter's exclusive use. Named for the *gatas* (cat-whiskered nurse sharks) that once lingered here, this beach is bordered by a long row of hewn rocks that create a breakwater. Snorkelers scope out the rocky coves, and surfers spring to life with the arrival of small but fun summer swells. The beach is lined with simple seafood eateries that provide lounge chairs for sunning, as well as kayak and snorkeling-gear rentals, and guiding services. (You really can't go wrong with any of the concessionaires, but La Red del Pescador, at the far end of the beach, has the most attractive setup with the hippest music; ask for Cruz if you need a kayak guide). Overlooking the beach is *El Faro* (the lighthouse); the view from the top is marvelous but the safe path up can be hard to find—ask any of the waiters to point it out. You can reach Playa las Gatas in about 20 minutes by climbing over the rocks that separate it from Playa la Ropa. But it's much more common and convenient to take one of the skiffs that run from the municipal pier every 10 or 15 minutes between 8 AM and a half hour before sunset. Buy your round-trip ticket (about $4) on the pier, and keep the stub for your return trip.

Playa la Madera. This is a small, flat, dark-sand beach with a sprinkling of restaurants on the sand (which provide just about the only shade, and facilities) and a few more hotels on or just above it. Bobbing boats and the green headlands make for beautiful vistas. Waves are small or nonexistent, and as there's no drop-off it's a great place for the kiddies. Young locals always seem to be kicking a soccer ball around. Get there via a footpath cut into the rocks that separate it from Playa Principal, in downtown Zihua, or by car.

Playa Principal. The less-than-pristine water (water taxis and fishing boats hang out here) may keep you on the sand, but there's plenty going on. Check out the haggling over fish prices, settle into an umbrella-shaded chair with a cool drink and fresh seafood, or shop at makeshift stalls for trinkets and treasures, but save the bulk of your beach-going time for other shores.

★ **Fodor'sChoice Playa la Ropa.** Playa La Ropa (Clothing Beach) apparently got its name hundreds of years ago when a textile-laden ship spilled its silks, which washed up on the sand. The area's most beautiful beach is a 20 minute walk from Playa la Madera and a five-minute taxi ride from town. Parasailers drift above the 1-km (½-mi) stretch of soft light sand; below, concessionaires rent Jet Skis ($40 for 30 minutes) and Hobie Cats (up to $50 an hour, depending on the size). Up and down the beach are open-air restaurants—some with hammocks for post-meal siestas—and a handful of hotels. Kids can splash in the calm, aquamarine water or toss a ball or Frisbee on the shore—but not too close to the little stream that empties into the southerly end: it's a crocodile refuge! There's free parking in a lot at the south end of the beach.

LAWN ORNAMENTS COME TO LIFE. See pink flamingos and other wading birds, head for Barra de Potosí (20–25 minutes south of the airport), where a beautiful laguna (lagoon) is an unofficial bird sanctuary. You can go on a tour or take a bus or taxi—you'll pay less for the latter, and you'll be able to linger at one of the casual restaurants lining the beach. Or, hire a fisherman's boat from Zihuatanejo's municipal pier or Playa La Ropa for a trip to the scenic, remote Playa Manzanillo, which is great for snorkeling.

WHERE TO EAT

IXTAPA

ITALIAN

$$$–$$$$ ✕ **Beccofino.** This small, marina-side dining room and cozy
★ bar has been a popular high-season hangout since 1992. Dark polished woods contrast with bright white linens, and bottles of wine are shelved on walls painted with trompe-l'oeil scenes. A canopy-sheltered deck overlooks the marina. Among the best dishes on the northern Italian menu are minestrone soup, *caprese* salad (with tomatoes, basil, and mozzarella), fish fillet (usually red snapper or mahimahi) with a champagne sauce, and chicken cacciatore. Many of the pastas are made in-house, and breakfast is available after 9:30 AM. Enjoy the personalized attention of the owner and all-around excellent service. ✉*Plaza Marina Ixtapa* ☎*755/553–1770* ⏱*Reservations essential* ▭*AE, MC, V.*

$–$$$ **MEXICAN**✕ **Casa Morelos.** The wooden bar, ocher walls, and handcrafted furnishings make this tiny restaurant seem like a true cantina, although it's in the middle of a shopping center. Patio tables are more elegant at night than during the day, with potted trees dressed in little white lights and lively tropical music at a level that doesn't drown out conversation. The chiles rellenos de camarón (egg-battered peppers stuffed with shrimp), fajitas, and tuna steak topped with three kinds of chiles are all filling and delicious. Or come early for a generous breakfast; the restaurant opens at 7:30 AM. ✉*La Puerta shopping center, Blvd. Ixtapa s/n* ☎*755/553–0578* ▭*AE, MC, V.*

CAFÉ

¢–$ ✕ **Nueva Zelanda.** Although it's open all day, this sparkling
☾ little coffee shop is best known for its breakfasts, which some say are the best in town. This branch opened after the success of the original eatery in downtown Zihuatanejo—and it's both more polished and more endearing.

Sit at the counter, at the varnished wood tables with six swivel chairs, or in the tiny booths. Options include fresh fruit juices, coconut milk shakes, banana splits, omelets, enchiladas, salads, soup, and *tortas* (sandwiches on large, crusty rolls). ⊠*Centro Comercial El Kiosko, behind bandstand, Blvd. Ixtapa s/n* ☎755/553–0838 ⚑*Reservations not accepted* ⊟*No credit cards.*

AMERICAN

¢–$ ✕**Ruben's.** The delicious scent of grilling meats will entrance
☺ you from blocks away. Latin music blares from the jukebox inside, so after sundown most clients dine at the white plastic tables on the grassy front yard. The charcoal-grilled burgers, which are made of top sirloin, and the french fries, deep-fried zucchini, and baked potatoes are true-to-the-source American treats. For dessert try the grilled bananas glazed with cinnamon and sugar and served with a dollop of fresh cream. ⊠*Centro Comercial Flamboyant, next to Bancomer bank, Blvd. Ixtapa s/n* ☎755/553–0027 *or 755/553–0358* ⊟*No credit cards.*

ZIHUATANEJO

ECLECTIC

$$$–$$$$ ✕**Kau-Kan.** When was the last time you enjoyed a plate of
★ stingray in black butter sauce? This unimposing restaurant encases the heart of Zihuatanejo's most deliciously inventive cuisine. Owner-chef Ricardo Rodriguez, who worked in Paris before returning to Mexico, applies deft Mexican and Mediterranean touches to seafood dishes in a beachcomber atmosphere overlooking the bay. The melt-in-your-mouth abalone and exquisite grilled mahimahi under a sweet, spicy pineapple sauce are popular choices, but the house specialty remains *patata rellena*—potatoes stuffed with shrimp and lobster in a fresh basil-and-garlic sauce. ⊠*Carretera Escénica, Lote 7 en route to Playa la Ropa* ☎755/554–8446 ⊟*AE, MC, V* ⊙*Closed last 2 wks of Sept. No lunch.*

CONTINENTAL

$$–$$$ ✕**Coconuts.** Eat at the horseshoe-shape bar—especially
★ if you happen to be by yourself—or out under the sky. Restored by owner Patricia Cumming's architect husband, Zihua's oldest house has a gorgeous patio open to the stars and surrounded by zillions of tiny white lights. The kitchen is consistent: try the roast pork loin, the sweet and zesty coconut shrimp, or one of the vegetarian offerings.

Five different dessert coffees are prepared flaming at your table. In the evening a keyboarder or romantic duo playing bossa nova or jazz is sure to entertain. ⊠*Pasaje Agustín Ramírez 1* ☎*755/554–2518* ⊟*AE, DC, MC, V* ⊘*Closed June–mid-Oct.*

SEAFOOD

$$$ ✕**Rossy's.** Waterside dining doesn't get any purer than at this spot in the midst of several beachfront eateries. The extensive menu covers all the typical favorites—ceviches, shrimp dishes, and fish fillets served with rice and steamed vegetables. Make a feast of it and choose the mixed-grill selection, which feeds three. For dessert, indulge in the crispy fried bananas served with a scoop of coconut ice cream or bathed in cinnamon-laced cream. Walk it off with a stroll along the sand. The people-watching is great, whether they're wearing swimsuits or business suits. ⊠*South end of Playa la Ropa* ☎*755/554–4004* ⊟*MC, V.*

$$–$$$ ✕**La Perla.** The slightly more-formal take on the typical toes-in-the-sand dining experience is evident in the fact this popular spot on Playa la Ropa accepts credit cards. Among the seafood specialties here are *filete* La Perla (fish fillet baked with cheese); lobster *thermidor*; and yummy fish or shrimp tacos made with homemade flour or corn tortillas and served with guacamole. There's a nice wine list and Havana cigars for after dinner. And, in fact, you don't have to get your feet wet or sandy at all; you can sit in the palapa-covered restaurant under the trees or take a stool at the corner bar, where there's always a game on satellite TV. But plenty of customers just sit on the beach and sip a drink. ⊠*Playa la Ropa* ☎*755/554–2700* ⊟*AE, MC, V.*

¢–$ ✕**Café America.** This small outdoor café is perfect for soaking up the boho vibe on a walking street lined with shops, small hotels, and huge potted plants. None of its hearty Mexican breakfasts costs more than $4. The lunch menu revolves around seafood plates and appetizers (try the *tiritas,* small strips of raw fish swimming in lime and onion) that don't top $5. Dinner is all about steak and lobster. There's an adjacent bar and rooms to rent upstairs. ⊠*Calle H. Galeana 16* ☎*755/554–4337* ⊟*No credit cards.*

MEXICAN

$$$ ✕**Casa Elvira.** This institution is right on the malecón, just a few steps from the fish market. It's not fancy, but the walls radiate bright orange, and a courtyard fountain splashes in a minor key. The staff is helpful yet unobtrusive, and the

food habitually good. The fare consists of Mexican dishes and such simple seafood plates as fish steamed in foil and served with rice and french fries. Lobster is a specialty, though it and the well-loved seafood platter will push your tab into the $$$$ category. ⊠ *Paseo del Pescador 32* ☎ 755/554–2061 ▭ MC, V ⊙ *Closed Tues.*

¢–$ ✕ **Doña Licha.** Come for the authentic Mexican dining experience. Stay for the televised soccer game or beauty pageant. Traditional dishes include barbecued ribs, goat stew, tripe, and on Thursday as Guerrero State tradition dictates— pozole. The long list of daily specials might include pork chops, tacos, and enchiladas—all come with a drink and either rice or soup. On the extensive regular menu are seafood and breakfast items. ⊠ *Calle de los Cocos 8, Centro* ☎ 755/554–3933 ▭ *No credit cards* ⊙ *No dinner.*

¢–$ ✕ **Tamales y Atoles Any.** The equivalent of a "soul food"
★ restaurant for Los Guerrerense (the people of Guerrero state), this noisy, fun spot a few blocks from the beach specializes in the traditional cuisine of the deep countryside. Tamales—16 different kinds—are the menu's most popular items. Ingredients ranging from pork and chicken to poblano peppers and squash blossoms are wrapped in *masa,* drenched in rich sauces and baked in corn husks or banana leaves. Pozole, a pork-and-hominy stew that is traditionally eaten on Thursday, is a specialty of the house. There's also a restaurant in Ixtapa at Centro Comercial los Arcos in front of the kiosk. Breakfast is served daily at the downtown Zihua location (in Ixtapa, daily except Sunday). ⊠ *Calle Vicente Guerrero 38, at Calle Ejido* ☎ 755/554–7373 ▭ MC, V.

WHERE TO STAY

IXTAPA

Ixtapa is great for getting sticker shock, especially during December and in mid-March, but winter vacationers can get some great deals at its priciest resorts in January after the New Year and most weeks in February. It definitely pays to see what deals sites like Expedia are offering and to get a price quote directly from the hotel to see if they're offering better prices than their Web site might imply. Ixtapa has several gated communities with condo and villa rentals; a good place to start is ⊕ *www.paradise-properties. com.mx.*

$$$$ ☎ **Barceló.** Once you get past its dull exterior, this high-rise
♻ turns out to be bright and lively. There's a subdued elegance
to its marble-floored lobby and an irresistible cheerfulness
to the skylighted inner courtyard—filled with a restaurant
and shops—where long vines hang from the balconies of
the surrounding rooms. The rooms are nothing special but
they are clean and comfortable; most have small balconies
with ocean views (be sure to request one and opt for a
higher floor to avoid noise from the pool area). The focus
is on the outdoors, from the beautiful pool and beach to
a sprawling list of recreational options, all facilitated by a
helpful staff. There's a quality live show six nights a week
and the hotel's Sanca Bar draws a nice crowd for dancing
to Latin music. **Pros:** Convenient to other hotels and restaurants, very social, lots of amenities and activities, good
service. **Cons:** Rooms need updating, very busy, restaurants
aren't spectacular. ⊠ *Blvd. Ixtapa s/n* ☎ *755/555–2000 or
800/227–2356* ⊕ *www.barcelo.com* ⇘ *341 rooms, 5 suites*
⚿ *In-room: safe, refrigerator. In-hotel: 4 restaurants, room
service, bars, tennis courts, pools, gym, spa, beachfront,
concierge, children's programs (ages 5–12), laundry service,
parking (no fee), no-smoking rooms, public Wi-Fi, public
Internet.* ⊟ *MC, V* ⊚ *AI.*

$$$–$$$$ ☎ **Las Brisas Ixtapa.** The balconies of this pyramid-shape
resort are reason enough to stay here—sunbathe or sip
cocktails from a deck chair during the day and stargaze
from your hammock at night (junior-suite balconies also
have hot tubs). Las Brisas is at the secluded southern end
of Ixtapa away from the main strip, so there's nothing but
blue water to gaze at. The resort is built into a hill and has
a bit of an awkward layout (it's kind of hike from the main
building to the pool complex), but who needs gardens to
stroll through when you're on the best stretch of beach in
Ixtapa? Recent refurbishments have turned the rooms into
the most attractive and modern looking of Ixtapa's resorts;
however, keep in mind that construction is still ongoing.
Standard rooms have low ceilings and are a little narrow,
but they have heavenly pillow-top beds and small sitting
nooks with comfy window-seat-like couches. **Pros:** Great
balconies and views, great beachfront, recently remod-
eled (July 2007), away from the hodgepodge of hotels on
the main strip. **Cons:** Lobby area is cavernous and not
that inviting, amenities and on-site restaurants are very
expensive, not within walking distance of main strip ($4
cab ride away). ⊠ *Playa Vista Hermosa* ☎ *755/553–2121
or 888/559–4329* ⊕ *www.brisas.com.mx* ⇘ *390 rooms,
26 suites* ⚿ *In-room: Safe, refrigerator, Wi-Fi. In-hotel: 6*

restaurants, room service, bars, pools, gym, beachfront, concierge, laundry service, public Internet, parking (no fee), no-smoking rooms. ⊟AE, MC, V ⊚EP.

$$–$$$ ⊞**Emporio Ixtapa.** Furnishings are an adroit mix of rustic and modern in this midsize, 11-story resort. Rooms are simple but bright, done in mostly white with a few earth-tone accents (be sure to ask for one that's been recently updated). Junior suites have views from both the living room and the bedroom. There aren't any private balconies, but windows that reach nearly from the floor to the ceiling open to the sea breezes. A children's pool with a slide lures kids away from the palm-shaded main pool, which has a swim-up bar. **Pros:** Calmer than the megaresorts on strip, good value, good spa services. **Cons:** Not all rooms have ocean views, some rooms need to be updated, mediocre restaurants (avoid the all-inclusive plan). ⊠Blvd. Ixtapa s/n ☎755/553–1066 or 866/936–7674 ⊕www.hotelesemporio. com ⤶197 rooms, 23 suites ⋄In-room: Safe, DVD (some), Wi-Fi (some). In-hotel: 3 restaurants, room service, bars, tennis courts, pools, gym, spa, parking (no fee), public Internet, public Wi-Fi, laundry service, no-smoking rooms. ⊟AE, MC, V ⊚AI, BP.

ZIHUA VS. IXTAPA. Zihua's singular hotels and gentle pace make for a more authentic Mexican experience. Ixtapa's brand-name resorts and compact hotel zone add up to a more predictable—some might say reassuring—vacation.

TRONCONES

This once-primitive surf spot along the rugged coast is still pretty remote, but a series of very comfortable—in some cases, luxurious—hostelries have sprung up along the road that traces the waterfront. Thankfully, most of these accommodations try to adapt themselves to the gorgeous environment, rather than the other way around. The focus is on the beautiful beaches and lush foliage. There is no high-end shopping district and most of the restaurants are in the hotels.

$$ ⊞**Casa Ki.** Each bungalow at this homey haven in the wilds of Troncones has a patio with hammocks, table, and chairs. There's also a house (for $185 a night), with a full kitchen, two bedrooms, two baths, and a long porch looking right onto the sand and waves. All guests have access to a communal kitchen and dining room, as well as barbecue facili-

ties. **Pros:** Cute, colorful bungalows, pleasant beachfront, nice grounds. **Cons:** Three-night minimum stay required, a little overpriced, no a/c in most rooms, which can get stuffy, not many services. ✉*Playa Troncones* ✏*A.P. 405, Zihuatanejo, 40880* ☎*755/553–2815* ⊕*www.casa-ki.com* ⤳*3 bungalows, 1 house* ♿*In-room: No a/c (some), no phone, Wi-Fi, refrigerator, no TV. In-hotel: Restaurant, beachfront, laundry service, parking (no fee), public Wi-Fi.* ⊟*No credit cards* ⛺|*BP, EP.*

$$ ⌘ **Hacienda Eden.** Gorgeous views of Manzanillo Bay, a
★ beach that has both a nice point break and calmer areas for swimming, and large, cheerful rooms have earned Hacienda Eden a loyal following. The property, which is surrounded by palm trees and gardens, has a two-story house with ocean-view rooms and hammock-filled terraces; one-room ocean-facing bungalows with patios; and newer air-conditioned suites that can accommodate families. Throughout you'll see beamed ceilings, Talavera tile details, and splashes of purple, yellow, and turquoise. The restaurant is one of the best on the beach. **Pros:** Nice beach that is good for swimming, great restaurant, great hosts. **Cons:** Only a few of the suites have a/c and fridges, place books up far in advance, oddly enough, they are closed during peak surfing season. ✉*Camino de la Playa s/n* ☎*755/553–2802* ⊕*www.edenmex.com* ⤳*6 rooms, 4 suites, 4 bungalows* ♿*In room: No a/c (some), no phone, no TV, Wi-Fi. In-hotel: Restaurant, bar, beachfront, public Wi-Fi.* ⊟*No credit cards* ⊙*Closed May–Nov.*

$$ ⌘ **Inn at Manzanillo Bay.** On a prime surfing point, the inn
☺ attracts surfers who are sick of roughing it. Accommodations are small bungalows thatched in palm, with screened windows and mosquito nets over the beds; built-in couches are outside the sliding-wooden doors. A communal eating area is overseen by a chef trained at the California Culinary Academy, who whips up burritos, burgers, and more complex Asian-Mexican fare. A small shop rents snorkel, surf, and Boogie-board gear and arranges fishing and surfing expeditions. Rooms are discounted 20% during surfing season (June to November). **Pros:** Faces a popular point break and has on-site board rentals, beach bum atmosphere without being too rustic, nice pool. **Cons:** Overpriced, some readers have complained about rude staff, strict cancellation policies. ✉*Camino de la Playa* ☎*755/553–2884* ⊕*www.manzanillobay.com* ⤳*10 rooms* ♿*In-room: Safe.*

In-hotel: 2 restaurants, bar, pool, parking (no fee), public Wi-Fi. ☐MC, V ⏹EP.

ZIHUATANEJO

$$$$ ☒ **Amuleto.** Local architect Enrique Zozaya has created an unlikely rustic luxury with this five-suite boutique hotel nestled almost undetectably into the hills above Bahía Zihuatanejo. It's as if Gilligan won the lottery. An open-air palapa suite is surrounded by four air-conditioned units, all of them exquisitely appointed with furnishings and decorations of elemental stone, ceramic, and wood. Each room has a small infinity plunge pool if you're not in the mood for the communal pool. The emphasis on tranquility prohibits intrusive technology; there's no TV, radio, or sound system. **Pros:** Good for a romantic getaway, attentive staff, removed from other major beach resorts. **Cons:** No beachfront (3-minute taxi ride), not many activities. ☒*Calle Escenica 9* ☎*755/544–6222, 213/280–1037 in U.S.* ⊕*www.amuleto.net* ⇔*5 suites* ☖*In-room: Safe, refrigerator, Wi-Fi, Ethernet. In-hotel: Restaurant, room service, bar, pool, laundry service, gym, public Wi-Fi, public Internet, no kids under 16, no elevator.* ☐MC, V ⏹BP.

WORD OF MOUTH. "La Casa Que Canta ... is small, private, decadent. I was married there, honeymooned there, and can't wait to go back! Get a private pool suite for the ultimate trip; you won't need to leave the room." –wish

★ **Fodor's**Choice ☒ **La Casa Que Canta.** The "House That Sings"
$$$$ clings to a cliff above Playa la Ropa. All guest quarters have lovely furnishings and folk art and generous patios with bay views; suites have outdoor living areas. Bathrooms are luxurious, as are such touches as flower petals arranged in intricate mosaics on your bed each day. The infinity pool seems to be airborne; tucked into the cliff below, a saltwater pool overlooks the surf. The restaurant serves guests breakfast and lunch; dinners here are more formal and are open to the public (reservations required). **Pros:** Secluded and quiet with lots of privacy, excellent food, great spa services. **Cons:** No direct access to beach (it's one block away), no elevator and lots of stairs, overpriced. ☒*Camino Escénico a Playa la Ropa* ☎*755/555–7000 or 888/523–5050* ⊕*www.lacasaquecanta.com* ⇔*21 suites, 2 villas* ☖*In-room: Safe, no TV, Wi-Fi, refrigerator. In-hotel: 2 restaurants, room service, bars, pools, gym, spa, concierge, laundry service,*

9

parking (no fee), no kids under 16, no elevator, public Wi-Fi. ⊟*AE, MC, V* ¡○¡*EP.*

★ **Fodor'sChoice** ▨**Tides Zihuatanejo (formerly Villa de Sol).** The
$$$$ main draws are striking rooms, with winning Mediterranean-Mexican architecture, and the spectacular location on perfect Playa la Ropa. Paths meander through gardens, passing coconut palms and fountains en route to the beach. Rooms are artistically and individually designed, with bright but not overpowering textiles and folk art; in some the adobe walls have been left white, while in others they've been painted pale shades of yellow or orange. All rooms have terraces or balconies; suites have private plunge pools. Service is downright deferential, with "beach butlers" delivering everything from sunscreen to pre-programmed iPods to your palapa. **Pros:** Beautiful semiprivate beachfront, outstanding service, standard rooms that actually stack up to the pricier suites. **Cons:** Meal plan required in high season, four-night minimum stay required year-round, hosts a lot of corporate events and weddings, very pricey for the area. ⊠*Playa la Ropa* ☎*755/555–5500, 866/905–9560 in U.S. and Canada* ⊕*www.tideszihuatanejo.com* ⌦*35 rooms, 35 suites* ⌂*In-room: Safe, DVD (some), Wi-Fi. In-hotel: 2 restaurants, room service, bars, tennis courts, pools, gym, spa, beachfront, no-smoking rooms, public Internet, public Wi-Fi, some pets allowed, no elevator.* ⊟*AE, MC, V* ¡○¡*EP, MAP.*

$$$ ▨**Hotel Cinco Sentidos.** Perched above La Ropa beach, this intimate property has some of the best views of the bay from its infinity-edge pool. An all-white motif is brightened by colorful throw pillows and terra-cotta accents, as well as a few whimsical touches, like cactus-shape lamps and sunburst or gecko wall ornaments. All rooms have terraces with ocean views and plunge pools. The Grand Suite has an open-air living room with even more expansive views of the water and surrounding countryside. **Pros:** Similar aesthetic to the Tides at half the price, pillow-top mattresses, very quiet. **Cons:** No direct beach access, no restaurant, no elevator and lots of steps. ⊠*C. Escencia 8* ☎*755/544–8098* ⊕*www.hotelcincosentidos.com* ⌦*5 suites* ⌂*In-room: Safe, refrigerator. In-hotel: Pool, public Wi-Fi, no kids under 14, no elevator.* ⊟*AE, MC, V.*

$$–$$$ ▨**Brisas del Mar.** This is almost as enchanting as any of
★ Zihua's luxury hotels at a price that won't haunt you when you get home. Rooms and services are comfortable, not

extravagant, but are presented with delightful touches at every turn. And there are many such touches in the property's intricate layout, from the lobby's stone floor and wicker ceiling to the staircases that wander the lush cliff-side grounds. Rooms have Talavera ceramic sinks in wooden surrounds, carved doors and furnishings from Michoacán, molded plastic bathtubs, and large balconies with hammocks; most have fabulous bay views. Situated on the beach, the stone-and-concrete-floored Bistro del Mar ($–$$$) offers simple, delicious Mediterranean food, a wonderful view, and a welcome breeze. **Pros:** All rooms have terraces (some of which have Jacuzzis) and water views, large bathrooms, nice pool. **Cons:** Some room layouts are cramped, only the junior suites are true bargains, no elevator and some steep stairs. ⊠*Calle Eva Sámano de López Mateos s/n, Playa la Madera* ☎*755/554–2142* ⊕*www.hotelbrisasdelmar.com* ⇆*28 rooms, 1 villa* ⌂*In-room: Kitchen (some), refrigerator (some), DVD (some). In-hotel: Restaurant, bars, pool, spa, beachfront, parking (no fee), no-smoking rooms, public Wi-Fi, no elevator.* ⊟*MC, V* ⏁*EP.*

$–$$ ⊞**La Quinta de Don Andrés.** Though the namesake owner of this small, sharp hideaway overlooking Playa Madera passed away in 2005, the family has stayed true to the founder's high standards. Room have pristine white walls and tile floors, and balconies. The little suites still have wonderful sitting areas, bedrooms, minipatios, and small dining areas (toasters, blenders, and coffeemakers available on request). **Pros:** Great views from most rooms, suites have fantastic terraces and are a great value, hotel is equidistant from downtown and Playa la Ropa. **Cons:** Popular with families, so can be noisy; pool is very small. ⊠*Calle Adelita 11, Playa la Madera* ☎*755/554–3794* ☎☎*755/553–8213* ⊕*www.laquintadedonandres.com* ⇆*4 rooms, 8 suites* ⌂*In-room: Kitchen (some), no a/c (some), refrigerator (some). In-hotel: Pool, beachfront, parking (no fee), no elevator.* ⊟*No credit cards* ⏁*EP.*

NIGHTLIFE

Outside of the resort bars and discos, Ixtapa's nightlife options are limited—unless you like hanging out at Señor Frog's. Zihua's pedestrian-only core is great for barhopping; it has many casual spots and most of the restaurants in this area serve drinks, too.

There's salsa, Cuban, or romantic music at **Bandidos** (⊠*Calle Pedro Ascencio 2, at Calle Cinco de Mayo, Zihuatanejo* ☎*755/553–8072*) Monday through Saturday (in low season call to confirm schedule). It's smack in the middle of downtown and almost as popular with locals as with travelers—both foreign and domestic. In the afternoon and early evening you can get drinks, snacks, and full meals at the bar and outdoor patio. The TV is usually tuned to sports, though the volume is turned way down.

Head for **Blue Mamou** (⊠*Paseo Playa la Ropa s/n, near Hotel Irma* ☎*755/544–8025*) for live blues, swing, and jazz; it's open nightly except Sunday. The bar, which opens at 7 PM, sometimes hosts private events; call ahead for the schedule. Soak up the booze with some grub: ribs, chicken, fish, sausage, yams, and coleslaw.

Capricho's Grill (⊠*Cinco de Mayo 4, Zihuatanejo* ☎*755/554–3019* ⊕*www.caprichosgrill.com*) has live music Thursday, Friday, and Saturday—usually world, Latin, flamenco, or jazz—and occasionally hosts special events, such as concerts during March's Guitarfest. You can dine in a lovely courtyard with palm trees and hanging lanterns, or enjoy snacks, cocktails, and wine, and a front seat for the performances from the lounge.

Piano Bar Galería (⊠*Blvd. Ixtapa s/n, Ixtapa* ☎*755/553–2025 or 888/738–4205 toll-free in the U.S.*) in the Hotel Dorado Pacifico, has a wonderful happy-hour pianist playing romantic songs nightly from December to April and July and August. **Sacbé** (⊠*Calle Ejido at Guerrero, Zihuatanejo*) is just far enough outside of the touristy downtown core to attract locals. The crowd at this trendy tri-level club is usually very young (it's a bit more mixed when hosting the odd live-music performance), but there are plenty of couches to lounge on if you're too intimidated to hit the dance floor. The music is a mix of the latest international and Mexican dance and pop hits. The cover is very reasonable (never more than $5).

El Sanka Grill (⊠*Calle Ejido 22* ☎*755/554–9358*) has musicians playing traditional Mexican songs from 7 pm to 9 PM to finish off a long day of serving delicious grilled meat and seafood.

THE MERMAID'S SONG. Though it's hardly a secret—it's one of the venues that hosts the Guitarfest in March—El Canto de la Sirena (⊠*Calle Colegio Militar, Zihuatanejo* ☎ No phone) is something of a hidden gem, if only because of its unlikely location outside of town by the main bus station. This local favorite is owned by a local legend, guitarist José Luis Cobo López, who performs most evenings. There's live music (and sometimes dancing) Tuesday through Saturday starting at 10 pm; jam sessions usually last until the wee hours.

SHOPPING

IXTAPA

Shopping in Ixtapa lacks traditional Mexican energy. Most stores are relegated to strip malls across from the hotels on Paseo del Palmar. There are boutiques, restaurants, pharmacies, and grocery stores, but everything seems to blend together. A ban on street and beach vendors restricts small merchants to a large handicrafts zone, **Mercado de Artesanía Turístico,** on the right side of Boulevard Ixtapa across from the Hotel Barceló. It's open weekdays 10–9 and has some 150 stands, selling handicrafts, T-shirts, and souvenirs.

★ One of the few stores that stands out from the rest is **La Fuente** (⊠*Centro Comercial Los Patios* ☎755/553–0812 ⊠*Centro Comercial a Puerta* ☎755/553–1733), with its huge assortment of women's resort wear as well as housewares and gifts. For silver jewelry, check out **Santa Prisca** (⊠*Centro Comercial Los Patios* ☎755/553–0709).

ZIHUATANEJO

Downtown Zihuatanejo has a compact but fascinating **Mercado Municipal** with a labyrinth of small stands on the east side of the town center, on Avenida Benito Juárez between Avenida Nava and Avenida González.

★ On the western edge is the **Mercado de Artesanía Turístico** (⊠*Calle Cinco de Mayo between Paseo del Pescador and Av. Morelos*), with some 250 stands selling jewelry of shell, beads, and quality silver as well as hand-painted bowls and plates, hammocks, gauzy blouses, T-shirts, and souvenirs. **Casa Marina** (⊠*Paseo del Pescador 9, at main plaza* ☎755/554–2373) houses a variety of excellent small shops selling Yucatecan hammocks, Oaxacan rugs, and a smattering of folk art. It's generally closed Sunday except when the cruise ships call.

9

JAVA FIX. The mountains of Guerrero State are home to many coffee plantations, and several shops in Zihuatanejo sell certified-organic, shade-grown blends. **Café Zihuatanejo** (*Cuauhtémoc 170* ✉ *C. Galeana, between Bravo and Ejido*) is the best-known retailer in town; the Cuauhtémoc location sells beans, while the Galeana branch is a full café.

Zihua's tiny nucleus has several worthwhile shops; most are closed Sunday. Shop for wonderful silver and gold jewelry at **Alberto's** (✉ *Calle Cuauhtémoc 15, across from Cine Paraíso* ☎755/554–2161 ✉ *Calle Cuauhtémoc 12, at Calle N. Bravo* ☎755/554–2162 ✉ *Plaza Galerías across from Hotel Dorado Pacífico* ☎755/553–1436). **Arte Mexicano Nopal** (✉ *Av. Cinco de Mayo 56* ☎755/554–7530) sells Mexican handicrafts, reproductions of ancient art, candles, incense, and small gifts. **Fruity Keiko** (✉ *C. Guerrero 5a* ☎755/553–2802) has a colorful yet tasteful selection of crafts from local artists, including jewelry and great handbags and beach bags.

In The Tides hotel, **Gala Art** (✉ *Playa la Ropa* ☎755/554–7774) exhibits and sells paintings, jewelry, and bronze, wood, and marble sculptures crafted by artists from throughout Mexico. **Lupita's** (✉ *Calle Juan N. Alvarez 5* ☎755/554–2238) has been selling colorful women's apparel—including handmade pieces from Oaxaca, Yucatán, Chiapas, and Guatemala—for more than 20 years. **Valentina** (✉ *Paseo del Pescador 18* ☎755/554–9223) sells jewelry and pewter pieces.

SPORTS & THE OUTDOORS

DIVING & SNORKELING

More than 30 dive sites in the area range from deep canyons to shallow reefs. The waters teem with sea life, and visibility is generally excellent. Experienced, personable PADI dive masters run trips ($65 for one tank, $80 for two) and teach courses at **Carlo Scuba** (✉ *Playa las Gatas, Zihuatanejo* ☎755/554–6003 ⊕ *www.carloscuba.com*). **Nautilus Divers** (✉ *Calle Juan N. Alvarez 30, Zihuatanejo* ☎755/554–9191 ⊕*www.nautilus-divers.com*) is operated by students of famed local NAUI master diver and marine biologist Juan Barnard. They offer one- and two-tank dives and night dives ($65, $75, and $60, respectively), as well as six-day certification courses.

Sunrise Tours (⊠*Paseo del Pescador 9, Zihuatanejo* ☎*044/755–100–5315 cell*) rents snorkel equipment, surf and Boogie boards, and kayaks, and provides tours to the best places to play with them. **El Vigia** (⊠*South end of Playa la Ropa* ☎*No phone*) rents snorkel gear and arranges boat trips to snorkel spots at Isla Ixtapa or Playa Manzanillo, about an hour's ride south.

FISHING

Right at the pier, **Cooperativo de Pescadores Azuela** (⊠*Paseo del Pescador 81, Zihuatanejo* ☎*755/554–2056*) has a large fleet of boats with VHF radios; some have GPS. The outfit charges $150 for trips in small, fast skiffs with up to four passengers or $250 for larger, more comfortable, albeit somewhat slower, craft. **Cooperativo Triángulo del Sol** (⊠*Paseo del Pescador 38, Zihuatanejo* ☎*755/554–3758*) offers day trips in boats from 26 to 36 feet. Prices are in the $150 to $350 range.

VIPSA (⊠*Hotel Las Brisas, Paseo Vista Hermosa, Ixtapa* ☎*755/553–2121 Ext. 3469*) is a reliable bet in the Ixtapa area, with boats that can handle four to six passengers; prices range from $300 to $450. **Whiskey Water World** (⊠*Paseo del Pescado 20, Zihuatanejo* ☎*755/554–0147, 661/310–3298 in U.S.* ⊕*www.ixtapa-sportfishing.com*) dispatches seven-hour expeditions in pangas ($190 for two people) and cruisers of 32 feet ($250–$350 for three–four people) and 38 feet ($350–$395 for six–eight people). It's run by Ed Garvis, an American expat in business in Zihua since 1997.

GONE FISHING. Anglers revel in the profusion of sailfish (November through March), black and blue marlin (May through January), yellowfin tuna (November through June), and mahimahi (November through January). Light-tackle fishing in the lagoons and just off the beach in pangas (skiffs) for huachinango (red snapper) is also popular.

GOLF

The **Campo de Golf Ixtapa (formerly Palma Real Golf Club)** (⊠*Blvd. Ixtapa s/n, Ixtapa* ☎*755/553–1163 or 755/553–1062*) has an 18-hole, par-72 championship course designed by Robert Trent Jones Jr. It abuts a wildlife preserve that runs from a coconut plantation to the beach; you may glimpse a gator while you play. Greens fees are $75. You must use either a caddy ($19) or a cart ($35). Club rental is available. Part of the Marina Ixtapa complex, the challenging 18-hole, par-72 course at the **Club de Golf Marina Ixtapa** (⊠*Ixtapa* ☎*755/553–1410*) was designed by Robert Von Hagge. Greens fees are $94 (including cart). Caddies charge $20, and you can rent clubs.

WATER PARKS

Delfiniti Ixtapa (⊠*Blvd. Ixtapa s/n, next to Best Western Posada del Real* ☎*775/553–2707* ⊕*www.delfiniti.com*) showcases dolphins in a huge pool who interact with paying customers—giving "kisses" and "hugs" and short rides (you hang onto their fins as they paddle around on their backs)—in exchange for food treats. Sessions ranging from $50 to $130 are organized and priced by the age of customers (three–adult) and time in the pool (17 minutes–45 minutes). Reservations are highly recommended—you can book online—especially if you have kids under 7, as there are limited time slots available.

Travel Smart Acapulco

PLANNING TOOLS, EXPERT INSIGHT, GREAT CONTACTS

WORD OF MOUTH

"I dress normally, not elaborately, I do not wear a camera on my neck, do not call attention to myself, and I use a "Pacsafe" purse that can't be cut off or slashed (you can Google that if you are interested, they make tummy pacs also). This makes me feel more secure, but honestly I was never bothered at all."

—emd

GETTING HERE & AROUND

We're really proud of our Web site: www.fodors.com is a great place to begin any journey. Scan Travel News for suggested itineraries, travel deals, restaurant and hotel openings, and other up-to-the-minute info. Check out Book It to research prices and book plane tickets, hotel rooms, rental cars, and vacation packages. Head to Talk for on-the-ground pointers from travelers who frequent our message boards. You can also link to loads of other travel-related resources.

▌ BY AIR

American has nonstop flights to Acapulco from Dallas, with connecting service from Chicago and New York. Continental has nonstop service from Houston and Newark. Mexicana's flights from Chicago, San Antonio, New York, and Los Angeles stop in Mexico City before continuing on to Acapulco. Aeroméxico has one-stop or connecting service from Atlanta, Chicago, Houston, Miami, and Orlando. US Airways has a nonstop flight from Phoenix.

Airlines & Airports Airline and Airport Links.com (⊕ www.airlineand airportlinks.com) has links to many of the world's airlines and airports.

Airline Contacts Aeroméxico (☎744/466–9109). **American** (☎744/466–9227). **Continental** (☎744/466–9063). **Delta** (☎01800/902–2100 toll-free in Mex-

ico). **Mexicana** (☎744/486–7587). **US Airways** (☎744/466–9257).

Airline Security Issues Transportation Security Administration (⊕www.tsa.gov) has answers for almost every question that might come up.

CHARTER FLIGHTS

Apple Vacations offers air-only and air-and-lodging deals to Acapulco, Cancún, Cozumel, Los Cabos, Puerto Vallarta, Huatulco, and Zihuatanejo from more than 200 U.S. cities.

Contacts Apple Vacations (☎800/828–0639 ⊕www.godream vacations.com). **Funjet** (☎888/558–6654 ⊕www.funjet.com).

AIRPORTS

Aeropuerto Internacional Juan N. Alvarez is 20 minutes east of the city.

Airport & Transfer Contacts Aeropuerto Internacional Juan N. Alvarez (☎744/435–2060). **Transportes Aeropuerto** (☎744/462–1095).

Note: Some airline toll-free numbers have a 001800 prefix—two zeroes before the "1"—rather than 01800, like most Mexican toll-free numbers. This is entirely correct: what it means is that your call is actually being routed to the United States and will be charged as an international call.

GROUND TRANSPORTATION

Private taxis aren't permitted to carry passengers from the airport to town, so most people rely on Transportes Aeropuerto, a special airport taxi service. The helpful English-speaking staff will help you get on your way. Look for the desk with the sign that says TAXIS on the walkway outside the terminal. Tell the attendant what hotel you want, buy your ticket, and follow the directions to reach the dispatcher, who will guide you to your transportation. The ride from the airport to the hotel zone on the strip costs about $8 per person for the *colectivo* (shared minivan) and starts at $26 for an authorized cab. The drivers are usually helpful and will often take you to hotels that aren't on their list. Tips are optional, but appreciated.

▌ BY BUS

Getting around Mexico by bus is no longer for just the adventurous or budget-conscious. First-class Mexican buses are generally timely and comfortable, air-conditioned coaches with bathrooms, movies, reclining seats with seat belts, and refreshments (first class or deluxe, known as *primera clase* and *de lujo* or *ejecutivo*). They take the fastest route (usually on safer, well-paved toll roads) and make few stops between points. Second-class vehicles (*segunda clase*) connect smaller, secondary routes; they also run along long-distance routes, often taking longer, local roads. They're tolerable (and air-conditioned), even for long distances, but are usually cramped and make

many stops. The class of travel will be listed on your printed ticket—if you see economico printed next to servicio, you've been booked on a second-class bus. At many bus stations, one counter will represent several lines and classes of service and mistakes do happen. For comfort's sake, if you're planning a long-distance haul buy tickets for first class or better when traveling by bus within Mexico. Bring snacks, a sweater, and toilet paper. Smoking is prohibited.

Tickets for first-class or better—unlike tickets for the other classes—can be reserved in advance; this is advisable during peak periods or on routes that only have one or two first-class departures each day. You can make reservations for many, though not all, of the first-class bus lines, through the Ticketbus central reservations agency. If you're unable to reserve online, buy your tickets at the station the day before you travel. The day of travel, ask your hotel desk to confirm that your bus still exists—even executive class buses can be canceled at the last minute.

ARRIVING & DEPARTING

Bus service from Mexico City to Acapulco is excellent. Grupo Estrella Blanca has first-class buses, which leave every hour on the hour from the Taxqueña station; they're comfortable and in good condition. The trip takes 4½–5 hours, and a one-way ticket costs about $30. Estrella de Oro also has deluxe service, called Servicio Diamante, with airplanelike reclining seats, refreshments, restrooms, air-conditioning, movies, and hostess service. The deluxe buses leave four times a day, also from the Taxqueña station, and cost about $48. Plus service (regular reclining seats, air-conditioning, and a restroom) on the same bus line costs $31. For the most part, plan to pay in pesos, although most of the deluxe bus services have started accepting credit cards such as Visa and MasterCard.

GETTING AROUND

Within Acapulco, one of the most useful buses runs from Puerto Marqués to Caleta, making stops along the way. Yellow air-conditioned tourist buses, marked ACAPULCO, run about every 15 minutes along this route. If you want to go from the zócalo to the Costera, catch the bus that says LA BASE (the naval base near the Hyatt Regency). It detours through Old Acapulco and returns to the Costera just east of the Ritz Hotel. If you want to follow the Costera for the entire route, take the bus marked HORNOS. Buses heading to Pie de la Cuesta or Puerto Marqués say so on the front. The Puerto Marqués bus runs about every 15 minutes and is always crowded. The fare is under $1. Scarlet-with-white-stripe buses are the most common but lack air-conditioning and are often packed. They follow the same routes listed above and are a few cents cheaper.

Contact Estrella de Oro (⊠Av. Cuauhtémoc 158, Old Acapulco, Acapulco ☎744/485–8705 or 762/622–0648 ⊠Av. Taxqueña 1320, Tlalpan, Mexico City ☎55/5549–8520).
Grupo Estrella Blanca (⊠Calle Ejido 47, Old Acapulco ☎744/469–2028 ⊠Av. Taxqueña 1320, Tlalpan, Mexico City ☎55/5628–5721).

▮ BY CAR

There are two absolutely essential points to remember about driving in Mexico. First and foremost is to carry Mexican auto insurance. If you injure anyone in an accident, you could well be jailed unless you have insurance. Second, if you enter Mexico with a car you must leave with it. In recent years the high rate of U.S. vehicles being sold illegally in Mexico has caused the Mexican government to enact stringent regulations on bringing cars into the country.

You must cross the border with the following documents: title or registration for your vehicle; a passport or a certified birth certificate; a credit card (AE, DC, MC, or V); a valid driver's license with a photo. The title holder, driver, and credit-card owner must be one and the same—that is, if your spouse's name is on the title or registration of the car and yours isn't, you cannot be the one to bring the car into the country. For financed, leased, rental, or company cars you must bring a notarized letter of permission from the bank, lien holder, rental agency, or company. When you submit your paperwork at the border and pay the $27 charge on your credit card, you'll receive a car permit and a sticker to put on your vehicle, all valid for up to six months. Be sure to turn in the permit and the sticker at the border prior to their expiration date; otherwise you could incur high fines or even be barred from entering Mexico if you try to visit again.

The fact that you drove in with a car is stamped on your tourist card (visa), which you must give to immigration authorities at departure. If an emergency arises and you must fly home, there are complicated customs procedures to face. If you bring the car into the country you must be in the vehicle at all times when it is driven.

ARRIVING & DEPARTING

The trip to Acapulco from Mexico City on the old route (Carretera Libre a Acapulco) takes about six hours. A privately built and run four-lane toll road is expensive (about $48 one-way) but well maintained, and it cuts driving time between the two cities to 4½ hours. Many people go via Taxco, which can be reached from either road.

GETTING AROUND

Rent a car if you plan on being in town for a few days and want to take side trips to Taxco and the coastal villages. If you plan to spend most of your time at the beach in front of your hotel, however, you don't need to rent a car. Taxis and buses can take you around the Costera, Old Acapulco, and Acapulco Diamante.

Renting a car costs around $60 per day, including insurance and unlimited miles. It doesn't take many taxi rides to add up to the same amount. Driving in Acapulco is like driving in any crowded big city in the United States. The traffic along the Costera can get heavy, but it moves, and street parking is competitive but not hard to find. Some parking spaces have meters that accept peso coins, others are completely free.

Major Agency Contacts Avis (☎800/288-8888). **Budget** (☎744/481-2433). **Dollar** (☎744/466-9493). **Hertz** (☎744/485-8947).

AUTO INSURANCE

You must carry Mexican auto insurance, which you can purchase near border crossings on the U.S. side, by mail, or via the Internet. Purchase enough Mexican automobile insurance to cover your estimated trip. It's sold by the day ($10 per day and up), and if your trip is shorter than your original estimate, some companies might issue a prorated refund for the unused time upon application after you exit the country. Baja Bound, Mexico Insurance Professionals, and Instant Mexico Auto Insurance are a few of the many online outfits that allow you to buy the insurance beforehand, but if you're approaching the border at almost any U.S.-Mexico crossing, you'll be overwhelmed by companies where you can buy the insurance on the spot. Sanborn's is a reliable company, has offices in almost every border town, and offers online options, too.

Be sure that you have been provided with proof of such insurance; if you drive without it, you're not only liable for damages, but you're also breaking the law. You could be jailed during investigations after an accident unless you have Mexican insurance. For this reason, after an accident many Mexicans might simply pull over, discuss things, arrive at an impromptu cash settlement on the spot if necessary, and continue on their ways.

Contacts Baja Bound (☎888/552-2252 ⊕www.bajabound.com). **Instant Mexico Auto Insurance** (☎800/345-4701 in U.S. and Canada ⊕www.instant-mex-auto-insur.com). **Mexico Insurance Professionals** (☎888/467-4639 ⊕www.mexpro.com). **Sanborn's Mexican Insurance** (☎800/222-0158 in U.S. and Canada ⊕www.sanborns insurance.com).

GASOLINE

Pemex (the government petroleum monopoly) franchises all of Mexico's gas stations, which you'll find at most junctions and in cities and towns. Gas is measured in liters. Some stations accept credit cards and a few have ATMs, but don't count on it—make sure you have pesos handy. Overall, prices run slightly cheaper than in the United States (at this writing, about 63 cents a liter or $2.34 a gallon). Premium unleaded gas (called *premium*), the red pump, and regular unleaded gas (*magna*), the green pump, are available nationwide, but it's still best to fill up whenever you can. Fuel quality is generally lower than that in the United States and Europe, but it has improved enough so that your car will run acceptably.

Gas-station attendants pump the gas for you and will also wash your windshield and check your fluids and tire air pressure, if you ask for these services. A 5- or 10-peso tip is customary, depending on the number of services rendered (even if they just pump the gas). Make sure the attendant resets the pump to "0" and that you're charged the correct price. For a receipt, ask for recibo. To ask the attendant to fill the tank, say "Lleno (YAY-noh), por favor."

PARKING

A circle with a diagonal line superimposed on the letter *E* (for *estacionamiento*) means "no parking." Illegally parked cars are either towed or have wheel blocks placed on the tires, which can require a trip to the traffic-police headquarters for payment of a fine. When in doubt, park in a lot instead of on the street; your car will probably be safer there anyway. Lots are plentiful although not always clearly marked, and fees are reasonable—as little as $1 for a half day or up to $1 or more an hour, depending on where in the country you are. Sometimes you park your own car; more often, though, you hand the keys over to an attendant. There are a few (very few) parking meters in larger cities; the cost is usually about 10¢ per 15 minutes.

ROAD CONDITIONS

Mexicans are generally skilled drivers, but they do drive very fast, even on twisting or very dark roads. Most of the newer highways have either designated lanes for slower vehicles or a paved shoulder that is wide enough for you to cruise in while letting the speed demons pass.

That said, Mexicans are in some ways more courteous than U.S. drivers—it's customary, for example, for drivers to put on their hazard lights to warn the cars behind them of poor road conditions, slow-downs, or upcoming speed bumps; oncoming cars may flash their lights at you for the same reasons. If you're trying to pass a slower-moving vehicle and the driver notices your efforts (you should put on your left blinker), often he or she will signal you with the left blinker when it's safe for you to pass. (When you do pass, just remember to check that none of the cars behind you have gotten the same idea first—it's not uncommon to see one speed up from the back of a long line of cars as soon as the coast is clear.) However, the lines delineating the various lanes are most often totally ignored; horns are leaned on constantly; and you must either pass or be passed. Yet, the most dangerous thing about driving in Mexico is the actual road conditions—the potholes, inexplicable placement of speed bumps, etc.

Watch out for drunk drivers especially around holidays and late at night. Unless you're very familiar with the terrain, it's best to avoid driving at night outside the city, where you can run into—literally—wandering cows, horses, or dogs, or unforeseen speed bumps at the entrance to small towns. The utter lack of visibility on country roads, even the well-traveled highways, will make even the most confident driver white-knuckled after a few hours. Bandits are generally run off if they start staking out cars or buses along major tourist routes, where tourists with expensive cameras and cash are known to pass by, but their rare presence is another reason to avoid night travel, erring on the side of caution.

There are several well-kept toll roads in Mexico—most of them two lanes wide; a few have four lanes. These *carreteras de cuota* (toll highways) are numbered and connect major cities or border areas. (*Cuota* means "toll road"; *libre* means "free," and such roads are often one lane, slower, and usually not as smooth.) Some excellent roads have opened in the past decade or so, making car travel safer and faster. These include highways connecting Acapulco and Mexico City. However, tolls as high as $40 one-way (most tolls start at $6–$8) can make using these thoroughfares expensive.

In rural areas roads range from good to poor: use caution, especially during the rainy season, when rock slides, flooding, and potholes may pose problems. Be alert to animals, especially untethered cattle and dogs, and to dangerous, unrailed curves. Note that driving in Mexico's central highlands may also necessitate adjustments to your carburetor. *Topes* (speed bumps, also called reductors) are common and are very large; occasionally, you'll see one that's actually been painted or fitted with reflectors, but usually they're just announced by a single yellow sign. Slow down when approaching a village, where you'll find the most topes, but be aware that you may encounter them in some strange locations, such as on straight stretches of highway where there are no visible hazards or reasons to reduce speed.

ROADSIDE EMERGENCIES

To help motorists on major highways, the Mexican Tourism Ministry operates a fleet of more than 250 pickup trucks, known as the Angeles Verdes, or Green Angels, easily reachable by phone throughout Mexico by simply dialing 078. The bilingual drivers provide mechanical help, first aid, radio-telephone communication, basic supplies and small parts, towing, tourist information, and protection. Services are free, and spare parts, fuel, and lubricants are provided at cost. Tips are always appreciated (figure $5–$10 for big jobs, $3–$5 for minor repairs). The Green Angels patrol fixed sections of the major highways twice daily 8–8 (usually later on holiday weekends). If you break down, pull off the road as far as possible, lift the hood of your car, hail a passing vehicle, and ask the driver to notify the patrol. Most bus and truck drivers will be quite helpful.

Emergency Service Contacts

Angeles Verdes (☎078, nationwide 3-digit Angeles Verdes and tourist emergency line). **Ministry of Tourism hotline** (☎55/3002–6300).

RULES OF THE ROAD

When you sign up for Mexican car insurance, you should receive a booklet on Mexican rules of the road. It really is a good idea to read it to avoid breaking laws that differ from those of your country. If an oncoming vehicle flicks its lights at you in daytime, slow down: it could mean trouble ahead. When approaching a narrow bridge, the first vehicle to flash its lights has right-of-way. One-way streets are common. One-way traffic is indicated by an arrow; two-way, by a double-pointed arrow. Look for these signs in cities and towns; they're sometimes oddly placed or otherwise hard to see. Other road signs follow the widespread system of international symbols.

In Mexico City, watch out for "*Hoy no Circula*" notices. Because of pollution, all cars in the city without a Verification "0" rating (usually those built before 1994) are prohibited from driving one day a week (two days a week during high-alert periods). Posted signs show certain letters or numbers paired with each day of the week, indicating that vehicles with those letters or numbers in their license plates aren't allowed to drive on the corresponding day. Foreigners aren't exempt. Cars with license plate numbers ending in 5 or 6 are prohibited on Monday; 7 or 8 on Tuesday; 3 or 4 on Wednesday; 1 or 2 on Thursday; and 9 or 0 on Friday. Cars whose license plates have only letters, not numerals, can't drive on Friday.

Mileage and speed limits are given in kilometers: 100 kph and 80 kph (62 mph and 50 mph, respectively) are the most common maximums, which are regularly exceeded by most drivers. A few of the toll roads allow 110 kph (68 mph). However, speed limits can change from curve to curve, so watch the signs carefully. In cities and small towns, observe the posted speed limits, which can be as low as 20 kph (12 mph). Seat belts are required by law throughout Mexico.

Drunk-driving laws are fairly harsh in Mexico, and if you're caught you'll go to jail immediately. It's hard to know what the country's blood-alcohol limit really is. Everyone seems to have a different idea about it; this means it's probably being handled in a discretionary way, which is nerve-racking, to say the least. The best way to avoid any problems is to simply not drink and drive. There's no right on red. Foreigners must pay speeding penalties on the spot, which can be steep; sometimes you're better off offering a little *mordida* (bribe, though don't refer to it as such) to the officer—just take out a couple hundred pesos, hold it out inquiringly, and see if the problem goes away.

If you encounter a police checkpoint, stay calm. These are simply routine checks for weapons and drugs; customarily they'll check out the car's registration, look in the backseat, the trunk, and at the undercarriage with a mirror. Basic Spanish does help during these stops, though a smile and polite demeanor will go a long way.

▌ BY CRUISE SHIP

Many cruises include Acapulco as part of their itinerary. Most originate from Los Angeles, San Diego, and Fort Lauderdale. Some of the reliable cruise lines visiting Acapulco are Carnival, Celebrity, Cunard, Crystal, Disney, Holland America, Norwegian, Oceania, Princess, Radisson Seven Seas, Royal Caribbean, and Sil-

versea. You can book through a travel agent or by contacting the cruise line directly. It always pays to check out the cruises online in advance.

Cruise Contacts Carnival Cruise Lines (☎305/599-2600 or 888/227-6482 ⊕www.carnival.com). **Celebrity Cruises** (☎305/620-6000, 800/221-4789, 800/668-6166 in Canada ⊕www.celebrity.com). **Crystal Cruises** (☎310/785-9300 or 888/722-0021 ⊕www.crystalcruises.com). **Cunard Line** (☎800/728-6273 ⊕www.cunardline.com). **Disney Cruise Line** (☎800/951-3532 or 888/325-2500 ⊕www.disneycruise.com). **Holland America Line** (☎206/281-3535 or 800/626-9900 ⊕www.hollandamerica.com). **Norwegian Cruise Line** (☎305/436-4000 or 800/323-1308 ⊕www.ncl.com). **Princess Cruises** (☎661/753-0000 or 800/774-6237 ⊕www.princesscruises.com). **Radisson Seven Seas Cruises** (☎954/776-6123 or 800/285-1835 ⊕www.rssc.com). **Royal Caribbean International** (☎305/539-6000 or 800/327-6700 ⊕www.royalcaribbean.com). **Silversea Cruises** (☎954/522-4477 or 800/722-9935 ⊕www.silversea.com).

▌ BY TAXI

Before you go anywhere by cab, find out what the price should be and agree with the driver on a fare. Tipping isn't expected, but a few extra pesos are always appreciated. Drivers will sometimes recommend a certain restaurant or store, from which they may get a kickback. That said, their recommendations can often be good ones, so if you're feeling adventurous, try one. Hotel taxis are the most expensive, the roomiest, and in the best condition. A price list that all drivers adhere to is posted in hotel lobbies. Fares in town are $3 to $7; from downtown to the Princess Hotel is about $18; from the hotel zone to Playa Caleta is about $9. Cabs that cruise the streets usually charge by zone, with a minimum charge of $2. A normal fare is about $3 to go from the zócalo to the International Center. Rates are about 30% higher at night. You can also hire a taxi by the hour or the day. Prices vary from about $10 an hour for a hotel taxi to $8 an hour for a street taxi; always negotiate. Minibuses travel along preset routes through Taxco and charge about 40¢. Volkswagen "bugs" provide inexpensive (average $1.50) taxi transportation.

ESSENTIALS

▍ ACCOMMODATIONS

▪TIP→**Find hotel and restaurant price charts in individual chapters.**

The price and quality of accommodations in Mexico vary from super-luxurious hotels and all-inclusive resorts to modest budget properties, down-at-the-heel places with shared bathrooms, and cabanas. There are far fewer *casas de huéspedes* (guesthouses) and youth hostels in Mexico than, say, Europe, because there are so many options for budget travelers. You may find appealing bargains while you're on the road, but if your comfort threshold is low, look for an English-speaking staff, guaranteed dollar rates, and toll-free reservation numbers. ▪TIP→**Assume that hotels operate on the European Plan (EP, no meals) unless we specify that they use the Breakfast Plan (BP, with full breakfast), Continental Plan (CP, continental breakfast), Full American Plan (FAP, all meals), Modified American Plan (MAP, breakfast and dinner), or are all-inclusive (AI, all meals and most activities).**

Fodors.com connection Before your trip, be sure to check out what other travelers are saying in *Talk* on www.fodors.com.

APARTMENT & HOUSE RENTALS

Contacts Vacation Home Rentals Worldwide (☎201/767–9393 or 800/633–3284 ⊕www.vhrww. com). **Villas & Apartments Abroad** (☎212/213–6435 or 800/433–3020 ⊕www.vaanyc.com). **Villas International** (☎415/499–9490 or 800/221–2260 ⊕www.villasintl.com). **Villas of Distinction** (☎707/778–1800 or 800/289–0900 ⊕www. villasofdistinction.com).

BOUTIQUE HOTELS & B&BS

Mexico has many unique properties that put you in close touch with the country's essence *and* cater to your need for pampering. Hoteles Boutique de México (Mexico Boutique Hotels) is a private company that represents 45 such properties. Most have fewer than 50 rooms; each is not only selected for its small size, service, and allure, but is inspected annually to ensure it continues to meet the set high standards. The bed-and-breakfast craze hasn't missed Mexico, although there are fewer than in Europe and the United States.

Reservation Services Bed & Breakfast.com (☎512/322–2710 or 888/782–9782 ⊕www.bedandbreakfast.com/mexico.html) also sends out an online newsletter. **Hoteles Boutique de México** (☎01800/508–7923 toll-free in Mexico, 877/278–8018 in U.S., 866/818–8342 in Canada ⊕www. mexicoboutiquehotels.com). **Mexperience Guide to Boutique Hotels** (⊕www.mexperience.com/mexico boutiquehotels).

HOSTELS

Mexico, while it has many cheap hotels, has few hostels. High school and college students are more often the norm than older travelers at the few hostels that do exist. HI has locations in Acapulco, Guanajuato, Guadalajara, Jalapa, Mexico City, and Puebla.

Information Hostelling International—USA (☎301/495–1240 ⊕www.hiusa.org).

HOTELS

It's essential to reserve in advance if you're traveling to the resort areas during high season or holiday periods, and it's recommended, though not always necessary, to do so elsewhere during high season. Overbooking is a common practice in some parts of Mexico, such as Cancún, Puerto Vallarta, and Acapulco. To protect yourself, get a confirmation in writing, via fax or e-mail. Travelers to remote areas will encounter little difficulty in obtaining rooms on a walk-in basis unless it's during a holiday, yet it's always wise to reserve if the property allows it.

Hotel rates are subject to the 15% value-added tax (it's 10% in the states of Quintana Roo, Baja California, and Baja California Sur, and anywhere within 20 km [12½ mi] of the border). In addition, many states charge a 2% hotel tax. Service charges and meals generally aren't included in the hotel rates.

The Mexican government categorizes hotels, based on qualitative evaluations, into *gran turismo*; five stars down to one star. Anything less than two stars generally doesn't advertise the fact, and even budget travelers are unlikely to stay at a one-star lodging. Keep in mind that many hotels that might otherwise be rated higher have opted for a lower category to avoid higher interest rates on loans and financing.

High- versus low-season rates can vary significantly. Hotels in this guide have private bathrooms with showers, unless stated otherwise; bathtubs aren't common in inexpensive hotels in smaller towns. Hotels have private baths, phones, TVs, and air-conditioning unless otherwise noted.

■TIP➔ **If you're particularly sensitive to noise, you should call ahead to learn if your hotel of choice is on a busy street.**

▮ COMMUNICATIONS

INTERNET

Internet cafés have sprung up all over Mexico, making e-mail by far the easiest and cheapest way to get in touch with people back home. If you're bringing a laptop with you, check with the manufacturer's technical support line to see what service and/or repair affiliates they have in the areas you plan to visit. Larger cities have repair shops that service Compaq, Dell, Macintosh, Sony, Toshiba, and other major brands, though parts tend to be more expensive than in the United States. Carry a spare battery to save yourself the expense and headache of having to hunt down a replacement on the spot.

Connections are fast in major cities and many smaller towns as well. Wi-Fi is widely available in many large hotels, at least in public areas. The cost for in-room connection can run from $15 to $25 per

LOCAL DO'S & TABOOS

CUSTOMS OF THE COUNTRY

In the United States and elsewhere in the Western world, being direct, efficient, and succinct is highly valued. But Mexican communication tends to be more subtle, and the direct style of Americans, Canadians, and Europeans is often perceived as curt and aggressive. Mexicans are extremely polite, so losing your temper over delays or complaining loudly will get you branded as rude and make people less inclined to help you.

Remember that things move at a slow pace here and that there's no stigma attached to being late; be gracious about this and other local customs and attitudes. In restaurants, for example, a waiter would never consider bringing you your check before you ask for it; that would be pushy. It's customary to inquire about a colleague's family or general health, and perhaps some other banal subject (such as the beauty of the town you're visiting, or the weather), before launching into a request or mundane business. Mexicans love to discuss politics and ethics, so don't be afraid to ask questions or discuss these issues in friendly and general terms.

Learning basic phrases in Spanish such as *por favor* (please) and *gracias* (thank you) will make a big difference in how people respond to you. Also, being deferential to those who are older than you will earn you lots of points.

GREETINGS

Mexicans are extremely polite and ceremonious. Businesspeople and strangers shake hands upon greeting each other or being introduced, while friends (women to women or women to men) may give a kiss on one cheek, or an "air kiss." Male friends or acquaintances may give each other a stiff hug with a triple pat on the back. When in doubt, shake hands.

It's traditional to use the formal form of you (*usted*) rather than the informal *tu* when addressing elders, subordinates, superiors, and strangers. However, so few gringos speak Spanish that any courteous attempt to speak Spanish is acceptable (although using the correct pronoun is, of course, best). When taking your leave, say *adios* (good-bye) or *hasta luego* (see you later).

SIGHTSEEING

Although shorts are permissible in churches, short shorts and skimpy tops are frowned upon. Don't sightsee during church services, although you can stand at the back and look. If photography and/or flash photography is prohibited, there's usually a sign at the front of the church; otherwise, taking pictures is not a problem. Old women and men or people with disabilities often beg at the entrance to churches; it's common to give them a few coins.

Say *con permiso* (pardon me) to get past people in a crowd.

Giving up one's seat on a bus for the elderly, blind, and pregnant women is common courtesy.

day—quite high, especially when Wi-Fi can sometimes be a free perk at other hotels. Many coffee shops in larger cities offer free Wi-Fi. Most Internet cafés charge 10 to 40 pesos for one hour, though some charge in 10- or 15-minute increments (usually 5 to 10 pesos). Many Internet cafés offer SKYPE connections, too.

Contacts Hostal K3 (⊠ Av. Costera Miguel Alemán 116, in front of Fiesta Americana hotel, Playa Condesa ☎ 744/481–3111). **Vid@ Net** (⊠ Calle Hidalgo off the zocálo, Old Acapulco).

PHONES

The good news is that you can now make a direct-dial telephone call from virtually any point on earth. The bad news? You can't always do so cheaply. Calling from a hotel is almost always the most expensive option; hotels usually add huge surcharges to all calls, particularly international ones. In some countries you can phone from call centers or even the post office. Calling cards usually keep costs to a minimum, but only if you purchase them locally. And then there are mobile phones *(⇨below)*, which are sometimes more prevalent—particularly in the developing world—than landlines; as expensive as mobile phone calls can be, they are still usually a much cheaper option than calling from your hotel.

The country code for Mexico is 52. When calling a Mexico number from abroad, dial any necessary international access code, then the country code, and then all of the numbers listed for the entry.

CALLING WITHIN MEXICO

Directory assistance is 040 nationwide. For assistance in English, dial 090 first for an international operator; tell the operator in what city, state, and country you require directory assistance, and he or she will connect you.

For local or long-distance calls, you can use either a standard public pay phone or a *caseta de larga distancia*, a telephone service usually operated out of a small business. To make a direct long-distance or local call from a caseta, tell the person on duty the number you'd like to call, and she or he will give you a rate and dial for you. Rates seem to vary widely, so shop around, but overall they're higher than those of pay phones. If using a pay phone, you'll most often need a prepaid phone card. If you're calling long distance within Mexico, dial 01 before the area code and number. For local calls, just dial the number; no other prefix is necessary.

Sometimes you can make collect calls from casetas, and sometimes you cannot, depending on the individual operator and possibly your degree of visible desperation. Casetas will generally charge 50¢–$1.50 to place a collect call (some charge by the minute); it's usually better to call *por cobrar* (collect) from a pay phone.

CALLING OUTSIDE MEXICO

To make an international call, dial 00 before the country code, area code, and number. The country code for the United States and Canada is 1, the United Kingdom 44, Australia 61, New Zealand 64, and South Africa 27. Be sure to avoid phones near tourist areas that advertise, in English, "Call the U.S. or Canada here!" They charge an outrageous fee per minute. If in doubt, dial the operator and ask for rates. AT&T, MCI, and Sprint calling cards are useful, although infrequently, hotels block access to their service numbers.

Access Codes AT&T Direct (☎01800/112–2020 toll-free in Mexico). **MCI WorldPhone** (☎01800/674–7000 toll-free in Mexico). **Sprint International Access** (☎01800/877–8000 toll-free in Mexico).

CALLING CARDS

In most parts of the country, pay phones (predominantly operated by Telmex) accept only prepaid cards (tarjetas Lada), sold in 30, 50-, or 100-peso denominations at newsstands, pharmacies, minimarkets, or grocery stores; coin-only pay phones are few and far between. There are pay phones all over the place—on street corners, in bus stations, and so on. They usually have two unmarked slots, one for a Ladatel (a Spanish acronym for "long-distance direct dialing") card and the other for a credit card. These are primarily for Mexican bank cards, but some accept Visa or MasterCard, though *not* U.S. phone credit cards.

To use a Ladatel card, simply insert it in the appropriate slot with the computer chip insignia forward and right-side up, and dial. Credit

is deleted from the card as you use it, and your balance is displayed on a small screen on the phone. You'll be charged 1 peso per minute for local calls and more for long-distance and international calls. Most pay phones display a price list and dialing instructions.

A *caseta de larga distancia* is a telephone service usually operated out of a store such as a *papelería* (stationery store) or other small business; look for the phone symbol on the door. Casetas may cost more to use than pay phones, but you tend to be shielded from street noise, as you get your own little cabin. They also have the benefit of not forcing you to buy a prepaid phone card with a specific denomination—you pay in cash according to the calls you make. Operators place the call for you.

MOBILE PHONES

If you have a multiband phone (some countries use different frequencies than what's used in the United States) and your service provider uses the world-standard GSM network (as do T-Mobile, Cingular, and Verizon), you can probably use your phone in Mexico—even semi-remote coastal areas seem to get excellent reception, though don't expect the same to be true in out-of-the-way mountain towns. Roaming fees can be steep, however: 99¢ a minute is considered reasonable. And overseas you normally pay the toll charges for incoming calls. It's almost always cheaper to send a text message than to make a call, since text messages have a very low set fee (often less than 5¢).

ant to make local ...er buying a new SIM ... that your provider may ...nlock your phone for you ... a different SIM card) and ...paid service plan in the des-...tion. You'll then have a local ...mber and can make local calls ...t local rates. If your trip is extensive, you could also simply buy a new cell phone in your destination, as the initial cost will be offset over time.

■TIP→**If you travel internationally frequently, save one of your old mobile phones or buy a cheap one on the Internet; ask your cell phone company to unlock it for you, and take it with you as a travel phone, buying a new SIM card with pay-as-you-go service in each destination.**

There are now many companies that rent cell phones (with or without SIM cards) for the duration of your trip. Receive the phone, charger, and carrying case in the mail and return it in the mailer. EZ Wireless, Daystar, and other companies rent phones starting at about $3.50 per day or $88 per month. Charges vary for incoming and outgoing calls, depending on the plan you choose.

Contacts Daystar (☎888/908–4100 ⊕www.daystarwireless.com) rents cell phones at $6 per day, with incoming calls at 22¢ a minute and outgoing at $1.20.

TOLL-FREE NUMBERS
Toll-free numbers in Mexico start with an 800 prefix. These numbers, however, are billed as local calls if you call one from a private phone. To reach them, you need to dial 01 before the number. In this guide, Mexico-only toll-free numbers appear as follows: 01800/123–4567. The toll-free numbers listed simply as 800/123–4567 are U.S. numbers, and generally work north of the border only (though some calling cards will allow you to dial them from Mexico, charging you minutes as for a toll call). Numbers listed as 001800/123–4567 are toll-free numbers that connect you from Mexico to the United States and are charged as international calls.

▮ CUSTOMS & DUTIES
Upon entering Mexico, you'll be given a baggage declaration form—you can fill out one per family. Most airports have a random bag-inspection scheme in place. When you pick up your bags you'll approach something that looks like a stoplight; hand your form to the attendant, press the button, and if you get a green light you (and the rest of your family) may proceed. If you get a red light, you may be subject to further questioning or inspection. Some regional airports have heightened security and all passengers are required to undergo a cursory bag inspection. You're allowed to bring in 3 liters of spirits or wine for personal use; 400 cigarettes, 25 cigars, or 200 grams of tobacco; a reasonable amount of perfume for personal use; one video camera and one regular camera and 12 rolls of film for each; and gift items not to exceed a total of $300. If driving across the U.S. border, gift items must not exceed $50. You

aren't allowed to bring firearms or ammunition, meat, vegetables, plants, fruit, or flowers into the country. You can bring in one of each of the following items without paying taxes: a cell phone, a beeper, a radio or tape recorder, a musical instrument, a laptop computer, and portable copier or printer. Compact discs and/or audio cassettes are limited to 20 total and DVDs to five.

Mexico also allows you to bring one cat or dog, if you have two things: 1) a pet health certificate signed by a registered veterinarian in the United States and issued not more than 72 hours before the animal enters Mexico; and 2) a pet vaccination certificate showing that the animal has been treated (as applicable) for rabies, hepatitis, distemper, and leptospirosis. For more information or information on bringing other animals or more than one type of animal, contact a Mexican consulate. Aduana Mexico (Mexican Customs) has an informative Web site, though everything is in Spanish. You can also get customs information from the Mexican consulate, which has branches in many major American cities as well as border towns. To find the consulate nearest you, check the Ministry of Foreign Affairs Web site, ⊕*portal.sre.gob. mx/usa*, select Consular Services from the menu on the left, and scroll down.

Information Aduana Mexico
(⊕www.aduanas.sat.gob.mx).

U.S. Information U.S. Customs and Border Protection (⊕www.cbp.gov).

▍ EATING OUT

Acapulco restaurants gamut from humble the-wall shacks, street s. *taquerías,* and American-style food joints to elegant, internationally acclaimed restaurants. Pric naturally, follow suit. To save money, look for the fixed-menu lunch known as *comida corrida* or *menú del día,* which is served from about 1 to 4 almost everywhere in Mexico. During the day, rely on standard regional dishes served in the hot food area of the local market, or *mercado.* Most of the archaeological sites have a café, at the least, and sometimes, a surprisingly good restaurant.

For information on food-related health issues, see Health below.

MEALS & MEALTIMES

You can get *desayuno* (breakfast) in *cafeterías* (coffee shops), of course, as well as snack bars and other establishments. Choices range from hefty egg-and-chorizo—ham—or beef dishes (the meat is usually shredded in with the scrambled eggs) to *chilaquiles* (a layered casserole with fried tortilla strips, tomato sauce, spices, crumbled white cheese, and sometimes meat or eggs) to lighter fare like bread rolls, yogurt, and fruit. Some cafés don't open until 8 or 8:30, in which case hotel restaurants are the best bets for early risers. Panaderías (bakeries) open early and provide the cheapest breakfast you'll find—a bag of assorted rolls and pastries will likely cost less than $1. *Comida* (lunch) is traditionally the big meal of the day, and set menus usually and/or salad, bread ... a main dish, one or ...shes, and dessert. Res-...geared toward travelers ...ve lighter fare, and cafés ...staurants serve soups, sal-...sandwiches, and pizza for ...se who don't want a full spread. ...*ena* (dinner) tends to be lighter; ...n fact, many people just have milk or hot chocolate and a sweet roll; *tamales* are also traditional evening fare. Many restaurants, however, including both tourist-oriented and local spots serve substantial, multi-course dinners.

Restaurants are plentiful and have long hours. (Note, however, that seafood places often close by late afternoon.) Lunch is usually served from 2 PM to 4 PM; Mexicans rarely go out to dinner before 8 PM, although many types of eateries in different price ranges are open throughout the day, with street vendors filling in the gaps and feeding the late-night crowds. More traditional restaurants may close on Sunday. This isn't a problem in major tourist areas, where plenty of good eateries are open daily. If you're visiting a small town, however, it's best to check with locals or the hotel staff to avoid going hungry.

Unless otherwise noted, the restaurants listed in this guide are open daily for lunch and dinner.

PAYING

Most small restaurants do not accept credit cards. Larger restaurants and those catering to tourists take credit cards, but their prices reflect the fee placed on all credit card transactions. Credit cards most often accepted are Master-Card and Visa, and to a slightly lesser extent, American Express.

For guidelines on tipping see Tipping below.

RESERVATIONS & DRESS

Regardless of where you are, it's a good idea to make a reservation if you can. In some places it's expected. We mention them specifically only when reservations are essential (there's no other way you'll ever get a table) or when they are not accepted.

For popular restaurants, book as far ahead as you can (often two weeks), and reconfirm as soon as you arrive. (Large parties should always call ahead to check the reservations policy.) Some restaurants have online reservations, but it's again wise to call ahead. We mention dress only when men are required to wear a jacket or a jacket and tie.

▌ ELECTRICITY

For U.S. and Canadian travelers, electrical converters aren't necessary because Mexico operates on the 60-cycle, 120-volt system; however, many Mexican outlets have not been updated to accommodate three-prong and polarized plugs (those with one larger prong), so to be safe bring an adapter. Blackouts and brownouts—often lasting an hour or so—are fairly common everywhere, particularly during the rainy season.

Consider making a small investment in a universal adapter, which has several types of plugs in one lightweight, compact unit. Most laptops and mobile phone chargers are dual voltage (i.e., they operate equally well on 110 and 220 volts), so require only an adapter. These days the same is true of small appliances such as hair dryers. Always check labels and manufacturer instructions to be sure. Don't use 110-volt outlets marked FOR SHAVERS ONLY for high-wattage appliances such as hair dryers.

Contacts Steve Kropla's Help for World Travelers (⌖www.kropla.com) has information on electrical and telephone plugs around the world

▌EMERGENCIES

In a medical emergency, **dial 065 or 066; for police 060.** If you need to call the police, choose the tourist police (in white shirts and black shorts) instead of the city police (in blue uniforms), who are sometimes less than scrupulous. Hospital Magallanes is the best choice should you need emergency medical care. For less serious needs, your hotel may have an on-site doctor. The Costera strip has several pharmacies.

Emergency Numbers Tourist Police (☎744/485-0490). **Red Cross** (☎744/445-8178 or 744/445-5911).

Foreign Consulates Canadian Consulate (⌖*Marbella Mall, Suite 23, Costera* ☎744/484-1305). **U.K. Consulate** (⌖*Acapulco Internationa Convention Center, Av. Costera Miguel Alemán 4455* ☎744/484-1735). **U.S. Consulate**

(⌖*Continental Plaza F Costera Miguel Alemán Costera* ☎744/469-0556).

General Emergency Contacts Ambulance Network (☎800/32 1966 in U.S. and Canada, 001800/010-0027 in Mexico⌖www.airambulancenetwork.com) **Global Life Flight** (☎01800/305-9400 toll-free in Mexico, 800/831-9307 in U.S and Canada⌖www.global-lifeflight.com). **Mexico Ministry of Tourism** (☎800/446-3942 in U.S., 01800/903-9200 toll-free in Mexico⌖www.sectur.gob.mx).**U.S. Overseas Citizens Services Center** (☎202/501-4444⌖www.travel.state.gov).

Hospitals Hospital del Pacífico (⌖Calle Fraile and Calle Nao 4, Costera ☎744/487-7161). **Hospital Privado Magallanes** (⌖Calle Wilfrido Massieu 2, Costera ☎744/485-6194).

▌HEALTH

RISKS

FOOD

In Mexico the major health risk, known as *turista,* or traveler's diarrhea, is caused by eating contaminated fruit or vegetables or drinking contaminated water. In places not geared to foreigners, don't eat raw vegetables that haven't been, or can't be, peeled (e.g., lettuce and raw chile peppers or piles of fresh cilantro, a common cause of turista); ask for your plate *sin ensalada* (without the salad). Avoid uncooked food and unpasteurized milk and milk products. Although fresh *ceviche,* made of raw fish (or scallops or

...d in lemon juice can be ...vary travelers heed the ...of the Mexican Depart- ...Health, which warns that ...ating in lemon juice does ...onstitute the "cooking" that ...uld make contaminated shellfish ...fe to eat. Also, if you choose to eat food from street stands, check that utensils and dishes are properly washed and dried (plastic sleeves cover plates at the most hygienic street stalls), and that the food is hot and fresh-looking when you buy it. Although much street food may be healthful and tasty, it's best to err on the side of caution.

Drink only bottled water (or water that has been boiled for at least 10 minutes) even when you're brushing your teeth. *Agua mineral* means mineral water, and *agua purificada* means purified water. Hotels with water-purification systems will post signs to that effect in the rooms; even then, be wary. Restaurants in resort destinations don't want their customers dropping like flies, and take necessary precautions. Stay away from ice, unless you're sure it was made from purified water; commercially made purified ice usually has a uniform shape and a hole in the center. When in doubt, especially when ordering cold drinks at untouristed establishments, skip the ice: *sin hielo*.

Mild cases of *turista* may respond to Imodium (known generically as loperamide), Lomotil, or Pepto-Bismol (not as strong), all of which you can buy over the counter; keep in mind, though, that these drugs can complicate more serious illnesses. You'll need to replace flu-ids, so drink plenty of purified water or tea; chamomile tea (*te de manzanilla*) is a good folk remedy, and it's readily available in restaurants throughout Mexico. In severe cases, rehydrate yourself with Gatorade or a salt-sugar solution (½ teaspoon salt and 4 tablespoons sugar per quart of water). If your fever and diarrhea last longer than three days, see a doctor—you may have picked up a parasite that requires prescription medication.

PESTS

An excellent brand of *repelente de insectos* (insect repellent) called Autan is readily available; do not use it on children under age two. Sprays (*aerosoles repelentes contra mosquitos*) don't always have the effective ingredients; make sure they do. If you want to bring a mosquito repellent from home, make sure it has at least 10% DEET or it won't be effective. If you're hiking in the jungle (or near standing water or even a patio restaurant edged in tropical plants), wear repellent and long pants and long sleeves; if you're camping in the jungle, use a mosquito net and invest in a package of *espirales contra mosquitos,* mosquito coils, which are sold in *ferreterías* or *tlalpalerías* (hardware stores) and also in some corner stores. Dengue fever is carried by mosquitoes, so be sure to use enough repellent as necessary to keep mosquitoes away.

You can call International SOS Assistance's U.S.–based phone number collect from Mexico.

POLLUTION

In the last few years Mexico has had to make tough choices between much-needed development and protecting the environment. In some places the rate of development has exceeded the government's ability to keep the environment safe. Some cleanup action is under way, after studies released in early 2003 indicated that waters near 16 resort areas contained high levels of pollution from trash, sewage, or industrial waste. Of the resorts—which included Acapulco, Puerto Vallarta, Puerto Escondido, and Huatulco—Zihuatanejo was considered the most polluted. Two factors reportedly contributed to the problem: the waters off its shores are in a bay where pollution is more apt to accumulate than it would in open waters, and this area in particular had difficulties properly treating its wastewater. The cleanup efforts have a long way to go. Polluted waters can give swimmers gastrointestinal and other problems; ask locals about where it's best to swim.

SUN

Caution is advised when venturing out in the Mexican sun. Sunbathers lulled by a slightly overcast sky or the sea breezes can be burned badly in just 20 minutes. To avoid overexposure, use strong sunscreens and avoid the peak sun hours of noon to 2 PM. Sunscreen, including many American brands, can be found in pharmacies, supermarkets, and resort gift shops. Mosquitoes are most prevalent in tropical coastal areas and in the south so it's best to be cautious and go indoors at dusk (called the "mosquito hour" by locals).

OVER-THE-COUNTER REMEDIES

Farmacias (pharmacies) are the most convenient place for such common medicines as *aspirina* (aspirin) or *jarabe para la tos* (cough syrup). You'll be able to find many U.S. brands (e.g., Tylenol, Pepto-Bismol), but don't plan on buying your favorite prescription or nonprescription sleep aid, for example. The same brands and even drugs are not always available. There are pharmacies in all small towns and on practically every corner in larger cities. The Sanborns chain stores also have pharmacies.

SHOTS & MEDICATIONS

According to the U.S. National Centers for Disease Control and Prevention (CDC), there's a limited risk of malaria, dengue fever, and other insect-carried or parasite-caused illnesses in certain rural areas of Mexico (largely, but not exclusively, rural and tropical coastal areas). In most urban or easily accessible areas you need not worry. However, if you plan to visit remote regions or stay for more than six weeks, check with the CDC's International Travelers' Hotline. Malaria and dengue are both carried by mosquitoes; in areas where these illnesses are prevalent, use insect repellent. Also consider taking antimalarial pills if you're doing serious adventure activities in subtropical areas. Don't wait until Mexico to get the pills; ask your doctor for medicine that combats even chloroquine-

...ains. There's no vac-
...nbat dengue. Talk with
...lth care professional to
...ne if vaccinations against
...d, Hepititis A, or Hepititis
...e a good idea for you.

IP INSURANCE

Consider buying trip insurance with medical-only coverage. Neither Medicare nor some private insurers cover medical expenses anywhere outside of the United States. Medical-only policies typically reimburse you for medical care (excluding that related to preexisting conditions) and hospitalization abroad, and provide for evacuation. You still have to pay the bills and await reimbursement from the insurer, though.

Another option is to sign up with a medical-evacuation assistance company. A membership in one of these companies gets you doctor referrals, emergency evacuation or repatriation, 24-hour hotlines for medical consultation, and other assistance. International SOS Assistance Emergency and AirMed International provide evacuation services and medical referrals. MedjetAssist offers medical evacuation.

Medical Assistance Companies AirMed International (⊕www.airmed.com).**International SOS Assistance Emergency** (⊕www.intsos.com).**MedjetAssist** (⊕www.medjetassist.com).

Medical-Only Insurers International Medical Group (⊕www.imglobal.com). **International SOS** (⊕www.internationalsos.com). **Wallach & Company** (⊕www.wallach.com).

▮ HOLIDAYS

Banks and government offices close on January 1, February 5 (Constitution Day), March 21 (Benito Juárez's birthday), May 1 (Labor Day), September 16 (Independence Day), November 20 (Revolution Day), and December 25. They may also close on unofficial holidays, such as Day of the Dead (November 1–2), Virgin of Guadalupe Day (December 12), and during Holy Week (the days leading to Easter Sunday). Government offices usually have reduced hours and staff from Christmas through New Year's Day.

▮ MAIL

The Mexican postal system is notoriously slow and unreliable; avoid sending packages through the postal service and don't expect to receive them, as they may be stolen. It's much better to use a courier service. If you're an American Express cardholder, you may be able to receive packages at a branch office, but check beforehand with customer service to find out if this client mail service is available in your destination.

Post offices (*oficinas de correos*) are found in even the smallest villages. International postal service is all airmail, but even so your letter will take anywhere from 10 days to six weeks to arrive. Service within Mexico can be equally slow.

To receive mail in Mexico, you can have it sent to your hotel or use *poste restante* at the post office. In the latter case, the address must include the words a/c Lista de

Correos (general delivery), followed by the city, state, postal code, and country. To use this service, you should first register with the post office at which you wish to receive your mail. The post office posts and updates daily a list of names for whom mail has been received. Mail is generally held for 10 days, and a list of recipients is posted daily.

Information American Express (⊕www.americanexpress.com/travel).

SHIPPING PACKAGES

Federal Express, DHL, Estafeta, AeroMexpress, and United Parcel Service are available in major cities and many resort areas. These companies offer office or hotel pickup with 24 hour advance notice (sometimes less, depending on when you call) and are very reliable. From Mexico City to anywhere in the United States, the minimum charge is around $30 for a package weighing about 1 pound.

Overnight Service Contacts Pegasus Express (✉Av. Costera Miguel Alemán 178, Costera ☎744/484–1076). **DHL** (✉Av. Costera Miguel Alemán 810, Fracc. Hornos, Old Acapulco ☎744/485–9567). **Mail Boxes, Etc.** (✉Av. Costera Miguel Alemán 40–3, Costera ☎744/481–0565).

Post Office Contacts Correos (Post Office ✉Av. Costera Miguel Alemán 215, Old Acapulco ☎744/483–1674 ✉Acapulco International Center, Av. Costera Miguel Alemán, Costera ☎744/484–8029).

■ MONEY

The prices given in this book nearly always been converted U.S. dollars because high-end hotels and heavily touristed areas often quote prices in U.S. dollars. Admissions and meal prices outside these areas will likely be quoted in pesos.

If you travel only by air or package tour, stay at international hotel-chain properties, and eat at tourist restaurants, you might not find Mexico such a bargain. If you want a closer look at the country and aren't wedded to standard creature comforts you can spend as little as $35 a day on room, board, and local transportation. Speaking Spanish is also helpful in bargaining situations and when asking for dining recommendations.

As a general rule when traveling in Mexico, always pay in pesos. Hotels almost always accept dollars but usually do not offer a good exchange rate. Many businesses, most restaurants (unless they're high-end or in major resort areas), market vendors, and most highway tollbooths do not accept dollars. If you run out of pesos, pay with a credit card or make a withdrawal from an ATM.

■TIP➔**Unlike their U.S. counterparts, Mexican banks may refuse torn bills, and for this reason merchants also may refuse them.**

WHAT IT COSTS	
Cup of Coffee	80¢–$1.50

...STS	
	$2.50–$5
...vich	$1.50–$2.50
...e-Mile Taxi ...de	$1.50–$3.50
Museum Admission	Free–$10 (average $8)

Prices throughout this guide are given for adults. Substantially reduced fees are almost always available for children, students, and senior citizens.

ATMS & BANKS

Your own bank will probably charge a fee for using ATMs abroad; the foreign bank you use may also charge a fee. Nevertheless, you'll usually get a better rate of exchange at an ATM than you will at a currency-exchange office or even when changing money in a bank. And extracting funds as you need them is a safer option than carrying around a large amount of cash.

■TIP➔ **PIN numbers with more than four digits are not recognized at ATMs in many countries. If yours has five or more, remember to change it before you leave.**

ATMs (*cajeros automáticos*) are widely available, with Cirrus and Plus the most frequently found networks. Rural towns often lack banking facilities. Unless you're in a major city, treat ATMs as you would gas stations—don't assume you'll be able to find one in a pinch (in smaller towns, even when they're present, machines are often out of order or out of cash).

Many, but not all, gas stations have ATMs. All airports have ATMs but many bus stations do not.

Before you leave home, ask what the transaction fee will be for withdrawing money in Mexico (it can be up to $5 a pop), and ask which particular banks offer the lowest fees (Bank of America, for example, advises its customers to use Santander). Be sure to also alert your bank's customer-protection division to let them know you will be using your card in Mexico—otherwise they may assume that the card's been stolen and put a hold on your account.

Many Mexican ATMs cannot accept PINs (personal identification numbers, *número de identificación personal* or NIP in Spanish) with more than four digits. If yours is longer, ask your bank about changing your PIN before you leave home. If your PIN is fine yet your transaction still can't be completed, chances are that the computer lines are busy or that the machine has run out of money or is being serviced. Don't give up.

For cash advances, plan to use Visa or MasterCard, as many Mexican ATMs don't accept American Express. Large banks with reliable ATMs include Banamex, HSBC, BBVA Bancomer, Santander Serfín, and Scotiabank Inverlat. (⇨*Safety, on avoiding ATM robberies.*)

CREDIT CARDS

Throughout this guide, the following abbreviations are used: **AE,** American Express; **D,** Discover; **DC,** Diners Club; **MC,** MasterCard; and **V,** Visa.

If you plan to use your credit card for cash advances, you'll need to apply for a PIN at least two weeks before your trip. Although it's usually cheaper (and safer) to use a credit card abroad for large purchases (so you can cancel payments or be reimbursed if there's a problem), note that some credit-card companies *and* the banks that issue them add substantial percentages to all foreign transactions, whether they're in a foreign currency or not. Check on these fees before leaving home, so there won't be any surprises when you get the bill.

■TIP→ **Before you charge something, ask the merchant whether or not he or she plans to do a dynamic currency conversion (DCC). In such a transaction the credit-card processor (shop, restaurant, or hotel, not Visa or MasterCard) converts the currency and charges you in dollars. In most cases you'll pay the merchant a 3% fee for this service in addition to any credit-card company and issuing-bank foreign-transaction surcharges.**

Dynamic currency conversion programs are becoming increasingly widespread. Merchants who participate in them are supposed to ask whether you want to be charged in dollars or the local currency, but they don't always do so. And even if they do offer you a choice, they may well avoid mentioning the additional surcharges. The good news is that you *do* have a choice. And if this practice really gets your goat, you can avoid it entirely thanks to American Express; with its cards, DCC simply isn't an option.

Credit cards are accepted tourist areas. Smaller, less sive restaurants and shops, ever, tend to take only cash general, credit cards aren't accept in small towns and villages, excep in hotels. The most widely accepted cards are MasterCard and Visa. When shopping, you can often get better prices if you pay with cash, particularly in small shops.

At the same time, when traveling internationally you'll receive wholesale exchange rates when you make purchases with credit cards. These exchange rates are usually better than those that banks give you for changing money. (Before you go, it doesn't hurt to ask your credit-card company how it handles purchases in foreign currency.) In Mexico the decision to pay cash or use a credit card might depend on whether the establishment in which you are making a purchase finds bargaining for prices acceptable, as well as whether you want the safety net of your card's purchase protection. To avoid fraud, it's wise to make sure that "pesos" is clearly marked on all credit-card receipts.

Reporting Lost Cards American Express (☎800/992-3404 in U.S., 336/393-1111 collect from abroad, 55/5326-2522 in Mexico ⊕www.americanexpress.com). **Diners Club** (☎800/234-6377 in U.S., 303/799-1504 collect from abroad ⊕www.dinersclub.com). **Discover** (☎800/347-2683 in U.S., 801/902-3100 collect from abroad ⊕www.discovercard.com). **MasterCard** (☎800/622-7747 in U.S., 636/722-7111 collect from abroad, 55/5480-

.co ⊕ www.mastercard.
(☎ 800/234-6377 in
799-1504 collect from
⊕ www.visa.com).

RENCY & EXCHANGE

xican currency comes in denom-
ations of 20-, 50-, 100-, 200-,
and 500-peso bills. Coins come in
denominations of 1, 2, 5, 10, and
20 pesos, and 10, 20, and 50 centavos (10 and 20 centavos pieces are
rarely seen, however). Many of the
coins and bills are very similar, so
check carefully.

U.S. dollar bills (but not coins) are
widely accepted in border towns
and in many parts of the Yucatán,
particularly in Cancún and Cozumel, where you'll often find prices
in shops quoted in dollars. Still, in
the majority of the country, even
in other resort areas, pesos are the
preferred (and many times, only)
accepted currency. At this writing, the exchange rate was 10.39
pesos to the U.S. dollar. Check with
your bank or the financial pages of
your local newspaper for current
exchange rates. For quick, rough
estimates of how much something
costs in U.S. dollar terms, divide
prices given in pesos by 10. For
example, 50 pesos would be just
under $5.

ATM transaction fees may be
higher abroad than at home, but
ATM currency-exchange rates are
the best of all because they're based
on wholesale rates offered only by
major banks. And if you take out
a fair amount of cash per withdrawal, the transaction fee becomes
less of a strike against the exchange
rate (in percentage terms). How-

WORST CASE SCENARIO

Worst Case Scenario All your
money and credit cards have just
been stolen. In these days of
real-time transactions, this isn't a
predicament that should destroy
your vacation. First, report the
theft of the credit cards. Then get
any traveler's checks you were
carrying replaced. This can usually be done almost immediately,
provided that you kept a record
of the serial numbers separate
from the checks themselves. If
you bank at a large international
bank like Citibank or HSBC, go to
the closest branch; if you know
your account number, chances
are you can get a new ATM card
and withdraw money right away.
Western Union (☎ 800/325-
6000 ⊕ www.western
union.com) sends money almost
anywhere. Have someone back
home order a transfer online,
over the phone, or at one of the
company's offices, which is the
cheapest option. The U.S. State
Department's **Overseas Citizens
Services** (⊕ www.travel.state.
gov/travel ☎ 202/501-4444) can
wire money to any U.S. consulate or embassy abroad for a fee
of $30. Just have someone back
home wire money or send a
money order or cashier's check to
the State Department, which will
then disburse the funds as soon
as the next working day after it
receives them.

ever, most ATMs allow only up
to $300 a transaction. Banks and
casas de cambio (money-exchange
bureaus) have the second-best

exchange rates. The difference from one place to another is usually only a few pesos.

Some banks change money on weekdays only until 3 (though they stay open until 5 or later). Casas de cambio generally stay open until 6 and often operate on weekends also; they usually have competitive rates and much shorter lines. Some hotels exchange money, but for providing you with this convenience they help themselves to a bigger commission than banks.

You can do well at most airport exchange booths, though not as well as at the ATMs. You'll do even worse at rail and bus stations, in hotels, in restaurants, or in stores.

When changing money, count your bills before leaving the bank or casa de cambio, and don't accept any partially torn or taped-together notes as they won't be accepted anywhere. Also, many shop and restaurant owners are unable to make change for large bills. Enough of these encounters may compel you to request *billetes chicos* (small bills) when you exchange money. It's wise to hoard a cache of smaller bills and coins to use at these more humble establishments to avoid having to wait around while the merchant runs off to seek change.

ATMs are the best places to obtain pesos; they're convenient and safe, and they offer the best exchange rates. You'll also find many *casas de cambio* (currency exchange offices) around the zócalo and along the Costera. Their hours are generally Monday–Saturday. Most banks are open week 9–3 and Saturday 9–1.

Banks Banamex (✉Av. Costera Miguel Alemán 38-A, Costera ☎744/484–3381). **Bancomer** (✉Av. Costera Miguel Alemán at Calle Laurel, Fracc. Club Deportivo, Costera ☎744/484–8055). **Bital** (✉Calle Jesus Carranza 7, Old Acapulco ☎744/483–6113).

Exchange Offices Casa de Cambio Austral (✉Av. Costera Vieja 3, Old Açapulco ☎744/484–6528). **Casa de Cambio Servicio Auxiliares Monetarios** (✉Av. Costera Miguel Alemán 88, Old Acapulco ☎744/481–0218). **Dollar Money Exchange** (✉Av. Costera Miguel Alemán 151, Costera ☎744/486–9688).

■TIP→**Even if a currency-exchange booth has a sign promising no commission, rest assured that there's some kind of huge, hidden fee. And as for rates, you're almost always better off getting foreign currency at an ATM or exchanging money at a bank.**

▮ PACKING

For resorts, bring lightweight sportswear, bathing suits, and cover-ups for the beach. Bathing suits and immodest clothing are inappropriate for shopping and sightseeing, both in cities and, to a lesser extent, in beach resorts. Keep in mind that Mexican men do not generally wear shorts except in beach cities and resorts, even in extremely hot weather. In winter the resort areas along the Pacific coast can get very cool at night;

e you have at least one
...ong pants and sweater
... jacket. Men will want to
...lightweight suits or slacks
...blazers; women should pack
...sses or pants suits. You'll need a
...ghtweight topcoat for winter and
...n all-weather coat and umbrella
in case of sudden rainstorms. The
sun anywhere in Mexico can be
fierce; bring a sun hat and sunscreen for the beach and for sightseeing. You'll need a sweater or
jacket to cope with hotel and restaurant air-conditioning. ■TIP→It's
a good idea to bring along tissue
packs in case you hit a place where
the toilet paper has run out.

▌ PASSPORTS & VISAS

A tourist visa is required for all
visitors to Mexico. If you're arriv-
ing by plane, the standard tourist
visa forms will be given to you on
the plane. They're also available
through travel agents and Mexican consulates, and at the border
if you're entering by land. You're
supposed to keep a portion of the
form. *Be sure that you do.* You'll
be asked to present it, your ticket,
and your passport at the gate when
boarding for departure.

A tourist visa costs about $20. The
fee is generally tacked on to the
price of your airline ticket; if you
enter by land or boat you'll have
to pay the fee separately. You're
exempt from the fee if you enter by
sea and stay less than 72 hours, or
by land and do not stray past the
26–30-km (16–18-mi) checkpoint
into the interior.

In addition to having your visa
form, you must prove your citizen-
ship. U.S. Homeland Security regulations require U.S. citizens of all
ages returning by air to have a valid
U.S. passport. Those returning by
land or sea are required to present
either a government-issue photo ID
and a certified copy of your birth
certificate or a U.S. Passport Card.
Soon only passports or U.S. passport cards will also be required.

Minors traveling with one parent
need notarized permission from
the absent parent. You're allowed
to stay 180 days as a tourist; frequently, though, immigration officials will give you less. Be sure to
ask for as much time as you think
you'll need up to 180 days; going
to a Mexican immigration office
to extend a visa can easily take a
whole day; plus, you'll have to pay
an extension fee.

U.S. Passport Information **U.S.
Department of State** (☎877/487–
2778 ⊕http://travel.state.gov/pass-
port).

U.S. Passport & Visa Expediters
**A. Briggs Passport & Visa Expedi-
tors** (☎800/806–0581 or 202/338–
0111 ⊕www.abriggs.com). **American
Passport Express** (☎800/455–
5166 or 800/841–6778 ⊕www.
americanpassport.com). **Passport
Express** (☎800/362–8196 ⊕www.
passportexpress.com). **Travel Document Systems** (☎800/874–5100
or 202/638–3800 ⊕www.traveldocs.
com). **Travel the World Visas**
(☎866/886–8472 ⊕www.world-visa.
com).

GENERAL REQUIREMENTS FOR MEXICO	
Passport	Required for Americans traveling by air. Soon will be required for entry by land or sea
Visa	Required for stays of longer than 72 hours ($20, included in price of airline or cruise ticket); valid for 180 days
Vaccinations	Typhoid and Hepatitis A recommended by the CDC
Driving	U.S. or Canadian driver's license suffices; Mexican auto insurance is required
Departure Tax	US$18–$29, generally included in price of airline ticket

RESTROOMS

Expect to find reasonably clean flushing toilets and running water at public restrooms in the major tourist destinations and at tourist attractions; toilet paper, soap, hot water, and paper towels are not always available, though. Keep a packet of tissues with you at all times. Although many markets, bus and train stations, and the like have public facilities, you usually have to pay about 5 pesos for the privilege. Gas stations have public bathrooms—some tidy and others not so tidy. You're better off popping into a restaurant, buying a little something, and using its restroom, which will probably be simple but

clean and adequately equi[p]. Remember that unless other[wise] indicated you should put your u[sed] toilet paper in the wastebasket ne[xt] to the toilet; many plumbing sys[tems] in Mexico still can't handle accumulations of toilet paper.

Find a Loo The Bathroom Diaries (⊕www.thebathroomdiaries.com) is flush with unsanitized info on restrooms the world over—each one located, reviewed, and rated.

SAFETY

Acapulco has been plagued by increased gang violence in the past year, though police presence in tourist areas of the city has also increased.

Mexico City's age-old problem of pickpocketing has been overshadowed by robberies at gunpoint. Other developments have been abductions and robberies in taxicabs hailed from the street (as opposed to hired from a hotel or taxi stand), and even robberies on city buses.

Reports indicate that uniformed police officers have, on occasion, perpetrated nonviolent crimes, and that there's a growing problem with people impersonating police officers, pulling over motorists, and extorting money or robbing them. The patronage system is a well-entrenched part of Mexican politics and industry, and workers in the public sector—notably police and customs officials—are notoriously underpaid. Everyone has heard some horror story about highway assaults, pickpocketing, bribes, or foreigners languishing in jails. These reports apply part to Mexico City and remote areas of Oaxaca and pas.

common sense everywhere: on't wear expensive jewelry, including watches you care about losing, and try not to act too much like a tourist. Keep your passport and all valuables in hotel safes, and carry your own baggage whenever possible.

Avoid driving on desolate streets, and don't travel at night, pick up hitchhikers, or hitchhike yourself. Robberies do occasionally occur on long-distance buses. Use luxury buses whenever possible (rather than second- or third-class vehicles), which take the safer toll roads. Think twice about urges to get away from it all on your own (even as a couple) to go hiking in remote national parks; women in particular shouldn't venture alone onto uncrowded beaches.

Use ATMs during the day and in big, enclosed commercial areas. Avoid the glass-enclosed street variety of banks where you may be more vulnerable to thieves who force you to withdraw money for them.

Bear in mind that reporting a crime to the police is often a frustrating experience unless you speak excellent Spanish and have a great deal of patience. If you're victimized, contact your local consular agent or the consular section of your country's embassy.

If you're on your own, consider using only your first initial and last name when registering at your hotel. If you carry a purse, choose one with a zipper and a thick strap that you can drape across your body; adjust the length so that the purse sits in front of you at or above hip level. Store only enough money in the purse to cover casual spending. Distribute the rest of your cash and any valuables (including credit cards and your passport) between a deep front pocket, an inside jacket or vest pocket, and a hidden money pouch. Do not reach for the money pouch once in public. Better yet, leave your passport and other valuables you don't need immediately in your hotel's safe-deposit box.

If you're traveling alone or with other women rather than men, you may be subjected to *piropos* (flirtatious comments). Dressing conservatively may deflect some of the attention—at the very least, you won't stand out as much in more traditional rural areas—but don't count on it. This type of harassment is rare in small rural towns; you'll encounter more of it in the big cities, most especially in heavily touristed resort areas. Your best strategy is to ignore the offender.

GOVERNMENT ADVISORIES

As different countries have different worldviews, look at travel advisories from a range of governments to get more of a sense of what's going on out there. And be sure to parse the language carefully. For example, a warning to "avoid all travel" carries more weight than one urging you to "avoid nonessential travel," and both are much stronger than a plea to "exercise caution." A U.S. government travel warning is more permanent (though not necessarily more serious) than a so-called public announcement.

The U.S. Department of State's Web site has more than just travel warnings. The consular information sheets issued for every country have general safety tips and entry requirements (though be sure to verify these with the country's embassy).

At this writing, crime, murder, and kidnapping are all down in Mexico, and a dozen accused drug lords have been extradited to the United States for prosecution. Only time will tell if these measures are successful. Luckily, travelers are generally unaffected by these troubles, and using the common sense that applies to any metropolitan area should keep you safe.

General Information & Warnings
U.S. Department of State (⊕www. travel.state.gov).

▎TAXES

Mexico has a value-added tax of 15% (10% in the states of Quintana Roo, Baja California, and Baja California Sur, as well as areas that are up to 20 km, or 12½ mi, from the border), called IVA (*impuesto al valor agregado*). It's often waived for cash purchases, or incorporated into the price. When comparing hotel prices, it's important to know if yours includes or excludes IVA and any service charge. Other taxes and charges apply for phone calls made from your room. Many states are charging a 2% tax on accommodations that's used for tour promotion.

▎TIME

Mexico has three time zones; most of the country falls in Central Standard Time, which includes Acapulco and is in line with Chicago. Baja California is on Pacific Standard Time—the same as California. Baja California Sur, Sonora, Chihuahua, Sinaloa, and most of Nayarit are on Mountain Standard Time. If you're staying in southern Nayarit and flying out of the Puerto Vallarta airport, note that Puerto Vallarta, in Jalisco state, is on Mountain time—an hour later than Nayarit time. Mexico switches to and from daylight saving time on the same schedule as the United States.

▎TIPPING

When tipping in Mexico, remember that the minimum wage is just under $5 a day and that maids, bellmen, and others in the tourism industry earn minimum wage. Waiters and bellmen in international chain hotels, for example, think in dollars and know that in the United States porters are tipped about $2 a bag; they tend to expect the equivalent. You should always tip using local currency whenever possible so that service personnel aren't stuck going to the bank to exchange dollars for pesos.

What follows are some guidelines. Naturally, larger tips are always welcome: porters and bellhops, 10 pesos per bag at airports and moderate and inexpensive hotels and

...os per person at expensive ...s; maids, 10 pesos per night ...hotels); waiters, 10%–15% of ... bill, depending on service, and ...ss in simpler restaurants (any-where you are, make sure a service charge hasn't already been added, a practice that's particularly common in resorts); bartenders, 10%–15% of the bill, depending on service, or 10 pesos per drink if you're not running a tab; taxi drivers, 5–10 pesos if the driver helps you with your bags only (taxi drivers are not commonly tipped in Mexico, and in any case, commonly overcharge tourists); tour guides and drivers, at least 50 pesos per half day; gas-station attendants, 3–5 pesos unless they check the oil, tires, etc., in which case tip more; parking atten-dants, 5–10 pesos, even if it's for valet parking at a theater or restau-rant that charges for the service. Restroom attendants should be tipped 5–10 pesos. In some cases, this is their only wage.

VISITOR INFORMATION

Tourism offices provide city maps and sightseeing advice. Procura-duría del Turista, the State Attor-ney General's Tourist Office in the Acapulco International Center, is open 9 AM–11 PM daily. The Taxco Tourism Office is open weekdays 9–2 and 5–8; Saturday 9–3.

TIPPING GUIDELINES FOR MEXICO	
Bartender	10 pesos per drink
Bellhop	10–20 pesos per bag

TIPPING GUIDELINES FOR MEXICO	
Coat-check Personnel	10 pesos per item checked unless there is a fee
Hotel Concierge	20–50 pesos or more
Hotel Doorman	10 pesos if he helps you get a cab
Hotel Maid	10–20 pesos per day
Hotel Room-Service	10–20 pesos per meal
Parking Attendant	5 to 10 pesos
Porter or Skycap at Airport or Bus Station	10–20 pesos per bag
Restroom Attendant	5 to 10 pesos
Tour Guide	10% of the cost of the tour or 50 pesos per half day
Valet Parking Attendant	10–20 pesos, but only when you get your car
Waiter	10 to 15%

Contact Mexico Tourism Board in the U.S. (☎800/446–3942 [44-MEXICO] in U.S. ⊕www.visitmexico. com). **Procuraduría del Turista** (✉Acapulco International Center, Av. Costera Miguel Alemán 4455, Costera ☎ 744/484–4416 ⊕www. visitacapulco.com.mx). **Taxco Tour-ism Office** (✉Av. de los Plateros 1, Taxco ☎762/622–6616).

INDEX

Index

NOTES

NOTES

NOTES

NOTES

NOTES

NOTES

NOTES

NOTES

NOTES

ABOUT OUR WRITERS

A former Fodorite-turned-free-lancer, Seattle-based **Carissa Bluestone** still works regularly on several Fodor's titles. Carissa is also a contributor at Concierge.com. She revised the chapter on Ixtapa & Zihuatanejo.

Sensing something fishy about Mexico City's bad rap, in 2005, **Grant Cogswell** thought he'd better check it out himself, fell completely in love with the place, and now lives there part-time. Grant's former life as a civic activist in Seattle is dramatized in director Stephen Gyllenhaal's forthcoming film Zioncheck for President. Himself a screenwriter/producer (Cthulhu, 2008), Grant also frequently contributes to Seattle's weekly *The Stranger*. He contributed to Where to Stay and Where to Eat and wrote Beaches and After Dark.

Jonathan J. Levin is a pop culture critic and fiction writer. He's lived in Israel and Mexico, holding such jobs as taco-stand worker, kibbutz dishwasher, and English teacher. An adamant follower of history in the making, he witnessed the mass political protests in Mexico City, and the 2006 riots in Oaxaca City. Jonathan contributed to Where to Stay and Where to Eat and wrote Welcome to Acapulco and Shopping.

Claudia Rosenbaum is a staff reporter for *Us Weekly* magazine and travels to Mexico frequently, often in hot pursuit of celebrities. In her spare time, she's a practicing attorney. Claudia speaks fluent Spanish, due to a childhood in Puerto Rico. She updated Side Trip to Taxco and Exploring Acapulco.